D0501050

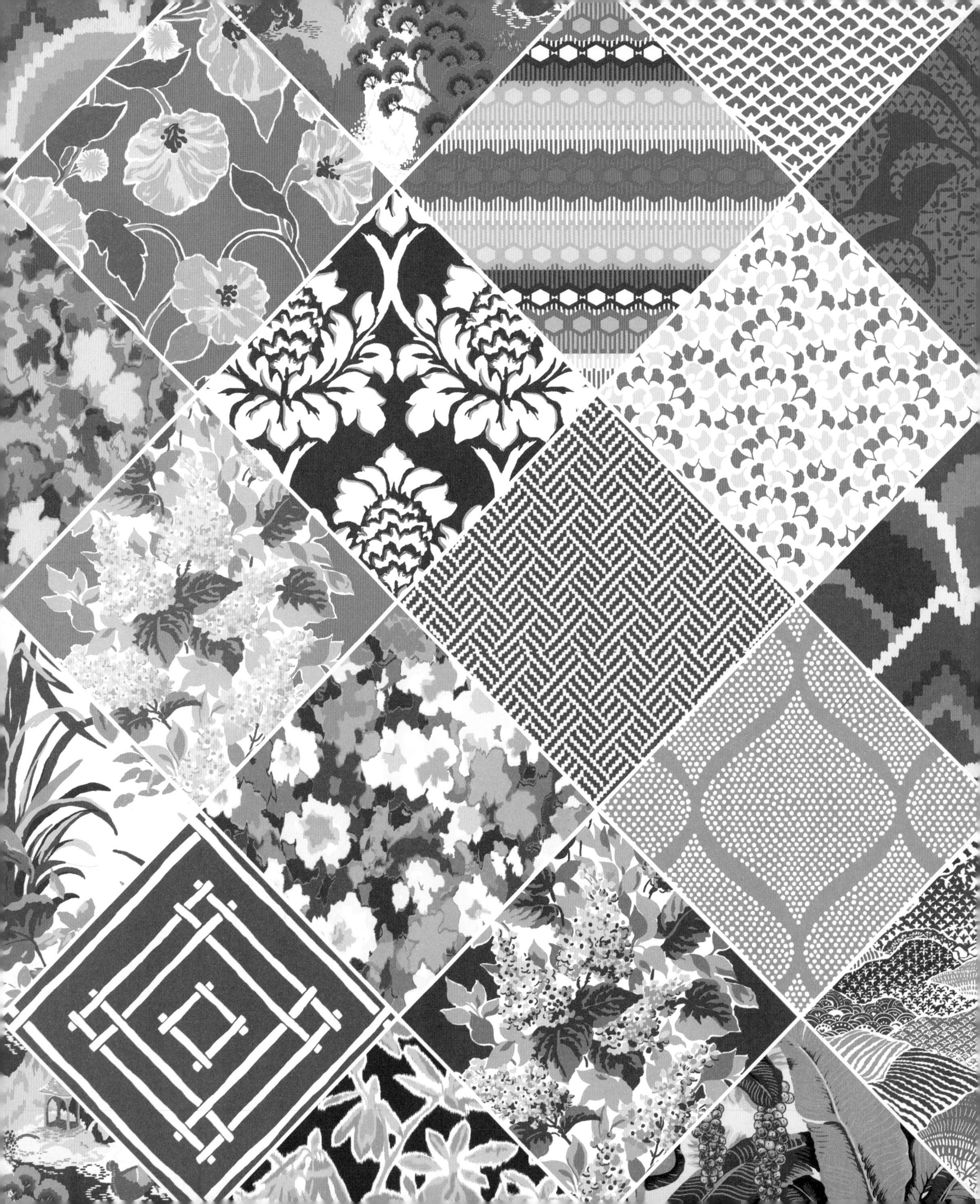

PRINTS
CHARMING

Create Absolutely Beautiful Interiors
with Prints & Patterns

MADCAP COTTAGE

John Loecke & Jason Oliver Nixon

PRINCIPAL PHOTOGRAPHY
BY JOHN BESSLER

ABRAMS, NEW YORK

1 *Pattern is* GUTSY

2 *Pattern is* TIMELESS

5 *Pattern is* MASCULINE

6 *Pattern is* PLAYFUL

The Original Prints Charming
CARLETON VARNEY

I FIRST MET JASON OLIVER NIXON almost twenty years ago, when he was editing a glossy lifestyle magazine in Palm Beach, Florida, and produced a fashion shoot with my line of colorful, print-driven resort wear. We stayed in touch and crossed paths over the years, meeting up for a cocktail or lunch at Michael's New York (a favorite lunch spot and watering hole for those in the media). I eventually made the acquaintance of the quiet, charming John Loecke when the gents came together to create their interior design and product development firm, Madcap Cottage. These boys know patterns like nobody's business and have created their own decorating style, a look of yesteryear glamour that's also decidedly right, right now. They combine the colorful treasures of a time gone by with a contemporary flair. I find their mix of pattern and color a new wave of what's new, now, next. There's no sterility for these gents; it's strictly *wow*. And it's fun, too.

I hope this book will give you good reason to consider a mix of fabulous prints and florals—and stripes, too!—in all your decorating plans.

Ride the wave. Enjoy!

—Carleton Varney

The Madcaps take
TEA WITH CARLETON V.

WE MET WITH CARLETON FOR TEA AT his Midtown East offices in Manhattan to discuss prints and pattern, paired with a delicious side of gossip. Think of these queries as our version of the Proust Questionnaire.

Varney is a Madcap Cottage hero, a legend of American design, and a visionary when it comes to interiors—and far-flung product lines—that sing with color, verve, and pattern. Varney began his interiors career in the early 1960s, working for Dorothy Draper & Company, Inc., and when the legendary Draper passed on, Varney picked up the baton and never looked back. High-octane commercial spaces are the specialty Chez Varney: Think the Greenbrier in West Virginia; Grand Hotel on Mackinac Island in Michigan; Dromoland Castle in Ireland; the iconic Colony in Palm Beach; and the US Ambassador's residence in Tokyo. Not to mention the Carter-era White House. Then there are his current product lines with Home Shopping Network (HSN) and Frontgate, his fabrics, his numerous books, and the CD compilations. . . . Whew! Plus, Varney is one of the nicest, most generous folk we know, and he can tell a great story that might involve past clients—Joan Crawford and Ethel Merman, let's say—while explaining how to reupholster a chair and give it some theatrical fun.

Madcap Cottage: What's your favorite tip for people scared of mixing patterns in their own homes?

Carleton Varney: Like [Franklin D.] Roosevelt said, "The only thing we have to fear is fear itself." People who never jump in the lake will never learn to swim. Just try it. You can always paint over or change things.

MC: What's your philosophy to mixing patterns in a room?

CV: Just go for it. I have a friend with twenty-five different pillow patterns upon a sofa, and it looks marvelous.

MC: What are your thoughts on the color beige?

CV: Dorothy Draper said, "Show me nothing that looks like gravy." There you have it.

MC: How should someone dip a toe into design if she is a newcomer to the world of pattern?

CV: Doing a room is not about furniture or about anything that people bring in or out. I always start with the walls and the ceiling and the view above the head. If you are going to do pattern, lay the patterns out on a table and see how they relate one to another in regards to color. Think of a garden and how you would build it. Everything is in levels in the garden, from hollyhocks in the background to the plantings in the foreground to the boxwood border that gives the structure. That's how you should construct a room.

MC: Florals or stripes? Or both?

CV: Together! Stripes are the decorating common denominator! Stripes work with everything and give a lift to rooms, heightening the space. I love a striped wallpaper and have been running stripes horizontally: Such a treatment works great in short hallways to make them feel long. As for florals, need you ask? I use them like mad anywhere I can.

MC: What's your favorite pattern?

CV: One of our patterns, Brazilliance [a heavenly tropical palm print packed with leafy luxe], my god, is an absolute classic. And I love a big openwork trellis.

MC: Any other advice you would like to share?

CV: Purchase quality over quantity. If you cannot afford the quality item, wait until you can. I would rather have nothing than something I know I will throw away.

Meet the
MADCAP COTTAGE GENTS

PUCKER UP AND SAY HELLO TO YOUR
Prints Charming (John Loecke, left, and Jason Oliver Nixon, right)! Once upon a time, in a faraway land, decorating was fun, rooms boasted pattern and color, and homes brought your personal storyline to life. . . .

Or was that only a fairy tale?

We hope not.

After all, decorating shouldn't be grim and glum. Interior design should be fun! It should be an adventure—one whose end result is rooms that burst with personality and that put a smile on your face the moment you step through the front door. But, sadly, this isn't always the case.

Somehow, along the road to decorating dreamland, many end up mired in the weeds, and the goal of crafting a uniquely personal space that sings with bespoke brilliance never quite materializes.

If this sounds like your home's storyline—and we suspect that it does, otherwise you wouldn't have picked up this book—know that there is hope. Your fairy godfathers (aka the Madcap Cottage gents) are here to help you turn that great old pumpkin of a home into a sparkling silver coach.

So what's the secret to taking a space and giving it new life? Patterns, friends, patterns. Today, spaces are more often than not vanilla—all white walls and neutral furnishings and accessories that lack a history or provenance. In short, your home looks like that of your neighbors and lacks any defining characteristics that truly make it your own. But help is at hand: It's time to dream big, kiss the frog, and transform your home with the wonders of pattern!

Certainly, our adventures in interior design have carried across numerous sensibilities and styles—from pattern that is romantic, peaceful, modern, over the top, and everything in between.

We are your Prints Charming, friends: We deftly shake up pattern to create interiors that overflow with fun and exuberance. We bend and break the rules and create a little magic in the process. As we like to say, "If it ain't broke, break it." But don't think that we are fancy or highfalutin—we get it. We understand budgets, we embrace reality, we drink red wine and spill occasionally, and we have pets and nieces and nephews who like to break out the Crayolas.

And, of course, the Madcaps love to talk design and embrace high design just as much as we enjoy shopping at flea markets and vintage stores and going on treasure hunts that carry us from Indiana to India and everywhere in between.

But let's talk about those charming prints and patterns. Did you know . . .

- Patterns can be romantic.
- Patterns can be peaceful.
- Patterns can be modern, playful, timeless, and everything in between.
- Patterns don't have to be florals or stripes—they can be wonderful textures and unexpected moments.
- Pattern can be soothing and cool. It does not have to be big, bold, and graphic, but it can be that, too.
- Florals do not have to be feminine. And they can serve as neutrals. Just keep them tonal.
- Texture is a pattern.
- Stripes and florals work swimmingly when paired together.

In all of our endeavors, we constantly discover that our clients and customers want to embrace the beauty of pattern. This book shows you how.

Take our former Brooklyn brownstone, for instance. Over the years, John and I moved up and down and sideways across Manhattan, from compact West Village walk-ups to carved-up brownstones on the Upper West Side. Each time we packed up our possessions, it was a question of needing more space: We had morphed from magazine editors to interior designers, and the business had followed us home, literally. As the design gigs started to roll in, each apartment grew successively smaller thanks to mushrooming fabric samples, paint swatches, and voluminous mood boards.

Our real estate agent, with whom we had worked on various moves, knew of our plight—and Anglophile tendencies—and rang us up one afternoon.

"It's a dream: a townhouse," she trilled. "A small slice of England on a charming dead-end street in an up-and-coming section of Brooklyn. And the price cannot be beat! Come take a look."

And so we trundled out to Brooklyn, a borough that, in 2005, wasn't the white-hot wonderland that it is today. Sure, we had visited the Brooklyn Academy of Music and Smith Street eateries on the odd occasion, but we had never considered decamping from Manhattan. We can recall many jokes over the years about passports and those pesky bridges and tunnels.

We turned off bustling Flatbush Avenue, a main Brooklyn artery (at the time, that section was all suburban hair salons and nail joints), and stepped into the city's version of the Cotswolds. The street, tiny Chester Court, boasted eighteen identical circa-1910 Tudor-style row houses and ended at an ornamented brick wall looking onto the Q train. Leafy Prospect Park was just around the corner, and the row house, well, it was huge—enormous, in fact—and had a tiny front yard in addition to a backyard that had heaps of potential. A dining room! A den! Multiple bathrooms! A basement that could become our office!

And so the Madcaps' Brooklyn adventure commenced. As did a yearlong renovation, which included less-than-sexy tasks, such as the addition of central air-conditioning and overhauls of the plumbing and electric.

And what element proffered the home's design magic? Pattern. And lots of it. From wallpapered ceilings to dressmaker details. From textured rugs to tiled walls.

From paint treatments to high-flying textiles and glorious art groupings. A guest bath nodded to the Beverly Hills Hotel with its frondy wallpaper and grass-cloth ceiling while the stairs layered artwork in all shapes and sizes with far-flung mats and frames. And it all worked swimmingly. In fact, we had to force guests to leave.

Think *GUTSY*, in all capital letters!

To learn more about how we packed this pad with heaps of punch, flip to Chapter 1.

This is no "Once upon a time . . ." story.

But it most certainly *is* "And they lived happily ever after (in their pattern-bedecked house)!"

Join us in the following pages and learn how to make that fabulous fairy tale your own reality. Pour yourself a cool cocktail, get comfortable, and see how pattern can make your life a little more interesting. Learn to layer in the florals, the textures, the details, and the fun, then throw a spirited dinner-and-disco party and watch your social life blossom like cabbage roses on an especially heady wallpaper.

Pattern is
EVERYWHERE

WE TRAVEL A LOT, AND OUR JOURNEYS carry us from our home base of High Point, North Carolina, on road trips up and down the East Coast (that's us in the Subaru Outback on I-95 with furniture strapped to every square inch of the roof and poking out the windows!) to long, languid weekends in the English countryside. We have shopped the markets in Oman, Turkey, and Egypt for exotic finds; we visit every house museum, castle, and royal retreat that Europe has to offer; and we love flea-market shopping in China (you haggle by plugging in a price in your cell phone, then the vendors counteroffer via phone, and you just keep passing the phone's calculator back and forth until everyone is happy). And we are constantly snapping photos of the glorious patterns that we encounter at every step of every journey. Keep your eyes open and your iPhone handy at all times, friends. It might be a detail on a building, a moment in a museum, a napkin at an eatery, or a floor pattern you find especially appealing. As legendary *Vogue* Editor in Chief Diana Vreeland said, "The eye has to travel," and the Madcaps are firm believers in this philosophy. Travel could be a walk through your neighborhood or a trip to the mall. Wonderful patterns are everywhere, and the ideas that you encounter can be brought home and into your living space. "My bathroom was inspired by the friezes upon the Parthenon," you can proudly tell your neighbors. "And I spotted a floral wallpaper at a hotel in West Virginia that transformed my upstairs hall. And the pattern on our basement rumpus room's ceiling came from a can of imported olives that I nabbed at Publix with two-for-one coupons."

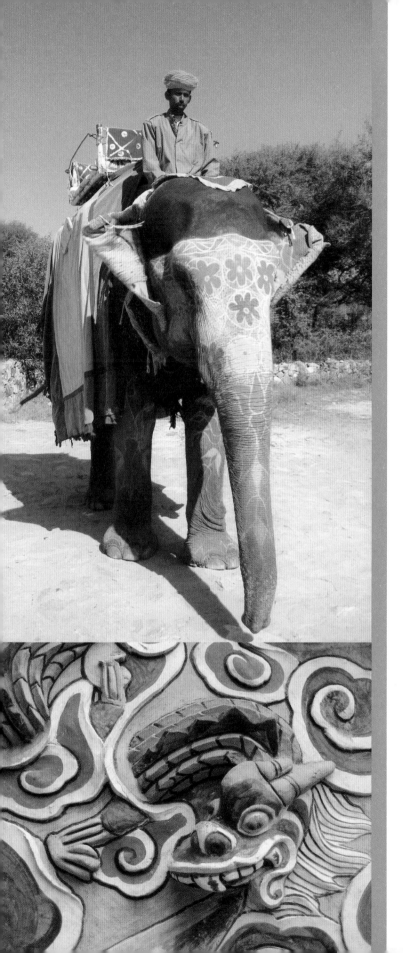

Inspired by
TRAVEL

THERE IS NOTHING THAT INFLUENCES our world more than travel, and that might be a jaunt to Iowa or India as much as a voyage to London or Los Angeles. We have said this before, and we'll say it again: Keep a notebook and your phone ready at all times. Are you lucky enough to be able to sketch and paint? If so, do as we do, and carry a mini set of watercolors in your purse or bag that you can break out in an especially inviting setting.

Moving right along. . . . Think of your own travel stories: What is it about a vacation or a hotel that you loved? Did you fall in love with a patterned fabric in a hotel bar in Mexico? Did the wallpaper in a Beverly Hills hotel's coffee shop make you swoon? Would you like to create a view in a room where the windows look onto a back alley? Have you always wanted to create an art arrangement like that museum in Florence or, perhaps, stack wonderful coffee-table books that will inspire you to travel, even if only in the armchair sense (a fabulous floral armchair, natch)? Then bring that experience home by wrapping a wall in wallpaper—whether a fantastic graphic or a grass cloth that you can embellish with artwork (grass cloth is great for hiding a misguided nail hole)—that will break the limitations of your home's architecture and give you visual interest where a view doesn't exist. At our previous home in Brooklyn, for example, we wallpapered a bathroom in a tropical palm-leaf pattern, and it felt like you had just packed up and taken a trip to St. Barts—without the need for a passport and sunscreen.

History
LESSON

PATTERN IS TIMELESS AND GLOBAL, FRIENDS!
Hello, Egypt and the pyramids and King Tut! Look to the past to find contemporary inspiration—whether that's a tour of the great palaces of Europe, a visit to Mexico City, or simply reading a book on the great designers of the past. The Madcaps are lucky enough to travel heaps, but we also collect vintage and current design and style books that have trained our eye and given our interior schemes context. If you hire us to design your home, we might reference a recent trip to Portugal and a sixteenth-century cathedral, a recent spread from *House & Garden* UK magazine, and a pattern we spotted on a wall at the Chrysler Building in Manhattan. Look to the past to move the needle forward.

Pattern is GUTSY

Interior design is about bringing **FANTASY** and a storyline to life: With a little vision and **INSPIRATION**, you can easily create an alternative reality in which to—quite literally—live. A landlocked home can be, on the inside at least, a breezy beach house. A house in the country can feel very **COSMOPOLITAN** and city chic. And a townhouse can become a small slice of England on a **CHARMING** dead-end street in an up-and-coming section of Brooklyn.

ONE TINY STREET JUST OFF FLATBUSH, the bustling Broadway of Brooklyn, boasts eighteen identical circa-1910 Tudor-style row houses and ends at an ornamented brick wall looking onto the subway. Stepping away from the honking horns and jostling, it feels like you have just been whisked away to the city version of the postcard-perfect Cotswolds region in England. Why not continue the neighborhood's British sensibilities inside the home?

The townhouse itself was large by New York City standards—multiple bedrooms and bathrooms, a dining room, a basement that could be an office—and full of potential. Our goal was to maintain the architectural integrity of the row house while imbuing it with color and pattern that would transform it into an English country house smack in the center of the city. We sought to make our home whimsical but sophisticated, timeless yet livable, grand but friendly in feel.

Chalk it up to pattern for making our vision a reality. From the living room, with its pink-trellis wallpaper-wrapped ceiling, to the dining room, which was modeled on Venice's fabled Gritti Palace hotel, to the exuberant florals of the guest room, the brownstone is awash in a plethora of pattern—florals, stripes, novelties, and graphics. The kitchen's mix of mismatched subway tiles pair with a scenic wallpaper and a wood-paneled ceiling, all sharing a fresh, soft green-and-yellow scheme. A guest bath, with palm-frond wallpaper and a grass-cloth ceiling, is a nod to Caribbean luxe by way of the Beverly Hills Hotel. The stairs, the connections between the divergent spaces and color palettes, boast expertly layered artwork—from large imposing portraits to small charming watercolors and everything in between—with far-flung mats and frames. The result is a look that is collected, personal, and full to the brim. Although each room is

filled with items and patterns that draw the eye—art, objects, furnishings, linens, wallcoverings, and rugs—nothing is jarring or out of place, just as a country house in the English countryside feels.

A curated art collection arranged in dense gallery formation, along with accessories that show decor should not be taken too seriously, provide the finishing touch. Follow our lead with your own decor and before you know it, friends will be coming to your house for holidays from their everyday lives. You might even have to pry them away.

opposite Bring a British invasion into your own home with pattern standards such as Jacobean-inspired botanicals in vivid hues that offer a lighthearted take on tradition.

Be brave, be bold, be gutsy! And never, ever be boring!

opposite Pink warms up spaces where light is at a premium (the two windows are north-facing). The striped floor is the perfect ground for the room's floral-upholstered seating and chinoiserie-patterned draperies. The wallpaper border adds interest beneath the crown molding. Jasper, our pound-rescue Boston terrier-boxer, takes it all in.

right Have fun with your art arrangements and groupings, and try a mix of frames with mat colors that take their hues from the art at hand.

If you want to be neutral, move to Switzerland.

left The long and narrow living room shines in Farrow & Ball's Fowler Pink paint and is lavished with trellis-pattern wallpaper overhead. Note how the coral hue extends from the walls to the ceiling wallpaper to the fabrics, a key tenet of pattern mixing: Ground a space in one color, then carry it throughout the room.

opposite Pattern upon a lampshade is an oft-overlooked detail that should be looked over far more often. This vintage Italian monkey wears a jaunty shade, with blossoms that relate to patterns on the sofa and the adjoining pair of armchairs.

this page The dining room is a jewel box of pattern and color, inspired by a favorite hotel bar in Venice. This delightful retreat brims with florals and flourishes, with bold blossoms spilling from the walls and onto the curtain panels and the upholstery of the vintage dining chairs (each chair has a different floral fabric). Black furniture adds the perfect neutral to the color cornucopia and bookends the room. And don't forget to bring pattern to the ceiling, too, such as the wallpaper treatment, pictured. A common theme—flowers—holds the scheme together.

*No one remembers
the shrinking violets. . .*

opposite Use painted furniture to carry a pattern story from fabrics and wallpapers onto three-dimensional pieces, such as mirrors and accessories. Takeaway: Layers bring depth and drama to a room. The mirror has a hand-painted chinoiserie motif that reflects the pattern of the drapery fabric, and the yellow-painted frame relates to the yellow wallpaper below the chair rail.

above Collect vintage linens and china, then pair your finds with items you own that share a similar story to create a table that's truly tip-top terrific.

right If your art budget is limited, invest in prints. These antique prints of garden buildings and plans are from London, but you can find similar treasures at flea markets and museum stores.

right Give a hardworking space—like a kitchen—personality and panache. Highlight color and pattern and have some fun. Wallpaper, yes! Pale green cabinetry, check! A mix of tiles, randomly installed, absolutely! Remember that pattern need not be limited to printed fabric or wallpaper.

opposite Why not paint the interior of your cabinetry a contrasting color to add some flair. These kitchen cabinets boast a sunny yellow interior. Think details, details, details—to surprise and delight.

*Pattern creates
fantasy where
none existed before.*

above Give a tired tabletop new life with an ever-changing selection of objects and accessories—from paperweights to boxes and vide-poches.

right Take an overlooked corner and make it something special with a grouping of artwork that boasts mismatched frames and matting treatments.

opposite There are over a dozen different motifs in this den, but the consistent color story—rich reds—ties it all together, from the keynote wallpaper with its brilliant lanterns to the statement-making area rug with its red tudor roses.

right Patterns and more patterns take center stage in the guest bedroom—and, yes, you can layer artwork upon a busy wallpaper. Brown wood furnishings help to ground the pattern riot. The theme that connects all sixteen patterns: florals.

opposite An antique painted secretary carries the floral motifs into a three-dimensional space and holds a collection of Egyptian pottery and other souvenirs.

Artwork gives your space instant sizzle and style.

above Strong color can anchor myriad patterns, and it need not be black or dark wood. Here, we used look-at-me yellow as a foundation, with a fretwork étagère showing the color proudly.

right Enjoy the journey! What was once a purely functional hallway is transformed into a dynamic art gallery courtesy of framed prints, photographs, and tea towels. The patterned display stands out from the textured grass-cloth walls.

opposite Pound-rescue pup Weenie relaxes on high-wattage Indian block-print cushions (chosen to play off the room's tree-of-life-patterned wallpaper). Modern artwork adds a contemporary spin.

this page Pattern makes the low-ceilinged third-floor master bedroom appear inviting and larger. Floor-to-ceiling color softens angles, while jaunty lattice wallpaper creates a focal point. The headboard, faux-bamboo floral bench, and bold Indian bedding pull the confection together.

left In the master bath, an Indian rug sets an unexpected tone. Why shouldn't a bathroom feel warm and inviting— with personal collections, artwork, and little luxuries.

opposite Look to tile to add pattern play into a space, such as the glass penny rounds in this shower. Note the floral Chinese garden stool used as a shower seat.

PROJECT
BEDTIME STORIES

YOUR BED IS THE PERFECT PLACE TO HAVE SOME fun—with sheets, quilts, blankets, shams, and decorative pillows, there are so many opportunities to apply pattern! You can easily add as much or as little as you like, without a lot of commitment. (When you fall in love with your delicious new bed, which you *will*, call us to design your toile-patterned sofa and wallpapered kitchen *tout de suite*!). After all, you spend one-third of your life in that California King, so why settle for boring beige linens that look like they came from a hospital?

But where to turn for brilliant bedding? Most department stores are a case study of the bland and blah, as they tend to offer white on white with nary a pattern or color in sight. And that's OK for the foundation of your bed, but sprinkle some candy—jimmies!—onto these vanilla underpinnings.

Decorative pillows gathered from your travels (these, pictured, hail from Guatemala and India) pair beautifully with a vintage textile masquerading as a duvet. This duvet is a crewelwork piece from Oman that our seamstress transformed into a top-of-bed stunner by backing it with a sheet and adding a zipper.

Layer multiple prints on your bed to bring a dash of visual interest. Note how rich greens pair perfectly with the soothing blues here. Thank the fabulous floral, trellis, and garden motifs for bringing the whole look together. And have fun with your pillows: Don't forget to mix European shams with standard pillows, and to layer bolsters with throw pillows. You'll feel like you've taken a mini vacation at a fantastic European hotel!

Go bold! This statement-making bed showcases heaps of Technicolor hues—from reds and corals to daffodil yellows to pinks and greens—and rich patterns—from roses and vermicelli stripes to embroidered botanicals, painterly animal spots, and ikats. Think of Fred and Ginger dancing across the silver screen in a fabulous setting in Hollywood's golden age. Your bed should make you feel the same way, only with a glass of wine in hand and a pile of trashy magazines in reach.

If luxe could kill. Use unexpected materials, such as cut velvet and silk, to add dimension and pattern to the bed. Decorative pillows made from cut velvet and a duvet crafted of silk lend delicious depth to this bed's silk-velvet headboard, and add a punctuation mark to the apartment's luxurious art deco theme.

bonus idea

SWEET DREAMS ARE MADE OF THIS The Madcaps are crazy about canopy beds, and we don't mean for your tween daughter who wants to be a princess. We mean for you! Canopy beds are a classic, timeless motif: We are thinking of two of our most favorite posh perches (both in London's sensational must-visit V&A Museum), the iconic Great Bed of Ware and the Chinese pagoda-shaped Badminton Bed. We cannot get enough of canopy beds, and we purchased two at auction that now take center stage in our own home (the bed shown here comes from the estate of actress Joan Fontaine).

TRADE SECRETS

stairway to heaven

The Madcaps believe that pass-through spaces should be savored, not overlooked. Take a foyer or a stairway, for instance, and cover it in artwork that you have picked up on your travels or with pieces painted by your kids. Think eclectic frames and matting treatments to amp up the pattern play and keep the eye constantly engaged. Layer photographs with paintings, prints with drawings, and sketches with ephemera, such as an old menu found at a flea market. The only rule: Have some fun! Grass cloth as a backdrop adds further texture and is terrific for hanging artwork.

sky's the limit

Wallpapering the ceiling is a favorite Madcap Cottage device. Why? Because wallpaper helps break a space out of its architecture, making it feel larger and masking architectural faults, while white ceilings actually make a room feel small and cramped. A big, bold pattern tricks the eye and creates the feeling that the ceiling is endless. Why shouldn't the fifth wall be especially engaging?

viva vintage!

Flea markets are great for finding vintage and antique furnishings and accessories, but also for unearthing vintage lighting. It's all about unique chic: Who wants lighting that is trendy and of the moment? Find someone who can rewire older pieces that need a little TLC. Hardware stores can often rewire vintage lighting, and you can find new harps, chandelier sleeves, and other accessories online. The Madcaps are addicted to colorful, fabric-covered electrical cord that we buy online, and we rewire all of our table and floor lamps in candy colors.

pet, set, go!

Take it from dapper Jasper, our pound-rescue Boston
terrier-boxer mix: Pets should be allowed in good decor
schemes! Patterned upholstery is a great way to hide minor
pet-related sins: choose fabrics with a high rub count
that can handle wear and tear. And don't forget about
prewashed slipcovers that can be thrown in the laundry.

WHY DON'T YOU

EMBELLISH YOUR WALLPAPER

with rhinestones and other "jewels." "Too much of a good
thing can be a very good thing," say the Madcaps.
Here, we festooned our Brooklyn dining room wallpaper
with wedding adornments—florals, paisleys, and more—
that we collected at markets in India and carried
home (a duffle bag full!). A glue gun, a little wine
to fuel the creativity, and voilà!

"I believe in doing the thing you feel is right. If it looks right, it is right."

—DOROTHY DRAPER

YOU OUGHT TO KNOW
DOROTHY DRAPER

THEATRICALITY! EXUBERANCE! COLOR!
Bold patterns! Check, check, check, and check. Step inside the Greenbrier resort, perhaps the greatest of iconic interior designer Dorothy Draper's still-existing commissions, and enter a wonderland where dramatic flourishes are de rigueur and persimmon walls lead into green (top and bottom) and then to red and yellow. Layer in baroque plasterwork, overblown camellias, and cabana stripes, and it's all W-O-W! And this in rural West Virginia, to boot! (Sorry, WV, but truly unexpected.) Draper grew up a blue-blooded WASP all the way but followed an unconventional path, becoming a trailblazing, independent, and shrewd design and business force who tackled everything from commercial properties (pay a visit to the lobby of the Carlyle in New York City, center) to furniture (the Braziliance Commode from Kindel Furniture, below), magazine columns (*Good Housekeeping*), and automobiles (*sigh*, bring back the Packards, *s'il vous plaît*) in a style she referred to as "Modern Baroque." Draper's signature splashy cabbage-rose chintz paired effusively with black-and-white checkered floors, lacquered doors, and exuberant plaster treatments that created high-octane architecture where none might already exist. Says Carleton Varney, our dear friend and the author of the book's foreword, who continues DD's spirited legacy, "Dorothy Draper was to decorating what Chanel was to fashion. She took a world that that was drab and dreary and made it colorful. The woman was a genius; there wouldn't be professional decorating businesses without her." Make a pilgrimage to the Greenbrier and prepare to enter candy land—and to live and breathe Draper's marvelous mantra, "Banish the beige!"

Your home should be like design ICON Iris Apfel and get more INTERESTING and ENGAGING with time.

Pattern is
TIMELESS

WHEN THE TIME comes for a new chapter in life, a historic 1920s-era **DUTCH** Colonial in a charming up-and-coming Midwest city might just fit the bill. Many times, however, the house isn't **PICTURE PERFECT**. Here, the home's history was top notch. But the 1980s-era kitchen and the wall-to-wall, top-to-bottom, Jayne Mansfield—esque, white **SHAG** carpet made the residence ready for an overhaul.

OUR MANDATE WAS TO CREATE A COOL, calm, and soothing environment that would repurpose many pieces of furniture inherited from parents and grandparents and give them a new chapter in which to shine.

Wallpaper? Yes, please! Pops of color? Absolutely!

The challenge: mixing together heirloom pieces from Marshall Field's and other great Chicago emporiums that, sadly, are no longer with us— whimsical and streamlined classic pieces (think great vintage films, such as *My Man Godfrey*) with sturdy farmhouse furnishings. It was a little like *Green Acres*, that classic TV show with Eva Gabor: One side of the family favored city life and the stores, the other, country living.

Naturally, we turned to pattern and color to bring the two sensibilities together.

And so we set off on a rollicking design plan that had us sending boxes filled with fabrics culled from Montmartre and the Left Bank of Paris and vintage furnishings from Palm Beach; taking farm furniture to a local painter in order to give the heaps of dark wood new life; and donating pieces that just wouldn't work. We repaired a rolled-arm sofa that was, for many decades, off limits to children; we scattered vintage plates that had been in the family for many years across walls to add luster; we scoured flea markets for the perfect ginger-jar table lamps; and we stenciled floors with oak-leaf patterns that mimicked those on the home's original exterior shutters. We developed a blue-and-white color scheme that paired Sister Parish and Manuel Canovas fabrics with classic American braided rugs, a splash of chinoiserie, built-in seating, a surprising backsplash behind the range, and a tiny casual breakfast room with heaps of impact.

Patterns in updated traditional florals, toiles, and foliage hold it all together with a common blue theme, giving the home a storyline and connecting the dots between the foyer and the living room, the kitchen and the master bedroom.

Updated traditional elements—including florals, toiles, and foliage—bring the pattern story together.

Create your own traditional look—complete with contemporary savvy—by renewing old furnishings with color, patterned upholstery, and a few updated accessories. Pair old and new with abandon. Be inspired by china patterns, and hang those plates as art. Choose a color scheme and stay true to it. The results are sure to be stunning!

Traditional never goes out of style, so invest in classic pieces such as Chippendale sofas and timeless wallpapers revved up with bold colors for a look that will only need to be refreshed as the years go by. Yes, just refreshed. Never start all over. Layer in pieces that will keep your look ever evolving: Leave cleaning house to the shows on TV, which aren't reality but rather reality television. Classic forms are smart and lively when paired with a mix of traditional and graphic patterns in familiar color schemes such as blue and green. Traditional moldings add appeal, too.

opposite The foyer is the first space that visitors encounter, and the natural jumping-off point for the home's pattern story. Use the foyer to set the scene for the house (here, a traditional Dutch Colonial full of classic, period-era details) with on-target design elements such as braided rugs, chinoiserie wallpaper, and bright colors that keep the scheme from feeling too trad. We suggest giving the "trad" a spirited dash of "rad."

Interior design should never be trendy, but rather on-trend.

left Blue-and-white chinoiserie wallpaper helps a petite entry tell a classic American tale. Chinoiserie was all the rage in England when the American colonies were settled and thus became a popular design motif in many stately colonial period homes.

opposite Use paint to enhance architectural elements. Here, painting the oval-shaped rosettes and the column insets of the Federal-style mantel makes these details truly stand out. The vine-and-floral-bouquet pattern in the rug echoes the blue-and-white pottery collection.

A bold pattern in an arresting hue creates a focal point and a warm, welcoming embrace.

left In the living room, a classic Duncan Phyfe—style sofa—an inherited heirloom—takes center stage. Like the foyer's chinoiserie wallpaper, the sofa's tree-of-life-patterned chintz is a design classic, with origins tracing to the China trade in the early 1700s. Tonal blue-and-white motifs round out the look and play off the flora and fauna elements in the chintz.

following spread, left Stumped about where or how to begin your own pattern transformation? Look to accessories for clues. Blue-and-white pottery figures prominently in this family's design aesthetic, so that gave us our *eureka!* moment.

following spread, right The blue-and-white color story carries from the wall and accessories onto the custom lampshade atop the fireplace mantel.

Turn to accessories that reference history for a look that is both traditional and timeless.

above How to give a vintage piece of furniture a fresh face? In the case of an upholstered chair, reupholster the frame in a graphic print. Here, the pattern on this classic armchair plays off the leaf elements found in the rug.

right The painted motif on the back of this eighteenth-century Italian chair inspired the choice of the bird-and-vine fabric used to refresh the chair's seat.

opposite Every room needs a bold pop of color to create a focal point. Here, the sofa's tree-of-life-patterned fabric has a touch of the oriental thanks to peony and lily blossoms paired with Asian-style birds in a look-at-me, rich red. The exotic flora and fauna help visually connect the sofa with the overscale and slightly more tropical pattern on the window treatments.

left Dark wood offers the perfect neutral tone to allow patterns to really sing—here, the blue-and-white chinoiserie just springs to life. In every room, choose at least one hue to anchor the pattern story.

opposite Strong, saturated colors, like the blue of the living room's walls and the black of this traditional table, are the perfect foils for the blue-and-white chintz draperies and the motif on the vase; they make these light and airy patterns pop. Notice the similarities between the pattern on the vase and that upon the curtain panels.

A tablescape is the perfect place to have some fun mixing patterns.

opposite The dining room and living room face each other on opposite sides of the foyer. The wall color of each room is the same, which connects the two spaces. There are other similarities, too, like the synergies of the dark wood and the floral-and-bird-print fabric. To give the eighty-five-year-old furniture a timeless look, we reupholstered the dining chair seats in a large-scale blue-and-white floral.

above Dip your toe into the world of pattern mixing and throw caution to the wind by setting your dining table with mismatched china. Not only is this an easy way to explore the power of pattern, it also will give your dining room a fresh look without a makeover.

right Pattern need not always be front and center. For example, the inlaid marquetry on this china cabinet supports the floral theme, but does so in a subtle fashion. A distinctive wood grain is another way to bring pattern into a room.

Pattern doesn't just have to be on your walls.

opposite A spirited oak leaf and acorn motif (inspired by the home's surroundings) and vintage blue-and-white plates continue the pattern story from the living and dining rooms.

above To give the utilitarian kitchen chairs a connection to the banquette's bold yellow hues, we painted the chairs' backs and stretchers and added cushions fashioned from a classic blue willow pattern fabric.

right A former butler's pantry becomes a cozy breakfast nook with a built-in banquette. The chair cushions have blue-willow-style patterns, referencing the collections of china and pottery throughout the house.

Bedding is an easy-breezy way to commit to pattern without purchasing a new sofa or papering over your walls.

this page In the second-floor master bedroom, blue-painted walls and a green-painted ceiling continue the color story from downstairs and help establish the palette for fabrics. Twin oval braided rugs, with alternating dark-and-light oval rings, add an energizing layer of pattern.

left When pairing fabrics, look for common design elements and similar materials. Here, the vine-patterned table skirt plays off the trailing florals on the drapery panels. Because both fabrics are cotton, they drape in a similar fashion and have similar visual weight.

opposite One of the tricks to successful pattern mixing is striking visual balance. In this bedroom, the multicolored floral on the chair corresponds with the multicolored floral used for the draperies. Meanwhile, the monochromatic vine pattern on the dressing table offsets the all-over green quilt covering the bed.

PROJECT
FLOOR SHOW

A LITTLE (OR A LOT OF!) PAINT IS A FANTASTIC WAY to take a tired floor and give it new life with pattern and playfulness. This could be a wood floor in a living room or a cement stretch in a former garage: Just do your homework on the appropriate paint for the floor at hand, sketch out a fantastic design, break out the painter's tape, and get to work. Stripes! Checkerboards! A herringbone or Greek key motif! (Only use colors that you will use elsewhere in the room once the space is pulled together.) In this Midwestern kitchen, the Madcap Cottage gents hand-stenciled oak leaves and acorns (inspired by trees in the home's neighborhood and a pattern lifted from the home's exterior shutters) to add visual interest to the newly blue-painted— and once reddish-stained—wood floor. Our goal was to give it a treatment that would be timeless yet packed with visual interest. Fifteen years later, the floor has held up swimmingly: Any wear and tear has only added luster. Plus, the stenciled floors bring much-needed pattern to a space that is largely white: The botanicals make what could have been a vanilla space warm and inviting. Do try this at home!

1

2

3

A decorative artist painted the fabulous Greek key motif that outlines the checkerboard-cum-stars pattern in this sophisticated foyer. After the floor was painted, we had it intentionally distressed so that dog toenails and the occasional scuff would only add further well-lived luster to the mix.

On a covered porch, rich chocolate- brown-and-white stripes—inspired by the foyer's bold wallpaper (see Chapter 3)— invite guests from the dining room into the great outdoors. Why should a porch floor be expected and unexceptional? Break out the tape and create some striped magic with a little imagination and some deck paint.

When a deluge damaged our parquet floors, we broke out the painter's tape and created a checkerboard pattern across the dining room with Farrow & Ball paint (expensive, but well worth it!). We then carried the high-gloss green shade up onto the baseboards and the moldings. Tip: Farrow & Ball paint has polyurethane mixed in so there's no need to seal it.

bonus idea

Don't overlook the treads and risers on the staircase in your home. Here, the Madcaps hand-stenciled risers with the same oak-leaf-and-acorn pattern found in the home's kitchen. The leaves seem to flutter in the breeze and give new life to a once-dull stairwell.

TRADE SECRETS

petal pushers

Fresh flowers offer a room that magical mix of texture and pattern lickety-split. We are especially partial to our local farmers' market and keep the flowers coming home through the summer and into the fall—from peonies to lilies to heaps of wildflowers and everything in between, sometimes adding a vine or branch from the yard. In the winter, we turn to a spot-on local florist who calls in flowers from all over the world. We love a good tightly bunched bouquet in an interesting patterned vessel that carries the pattern play through to every detail. Have fun with your floral displays; there are no rules. Really.

cool, calm, collected

Let a collection inspire your color palette. In this home, the owner collected vintage and antique blue-and-white china, and that set the scene for the entire house. It's sort of like shopping your closet for hues and patterns that you especially like: If you cannot figure out a color- or pattern-way in your home, sort through what you collect and look at your clothes, handbags, and shoes to seek inspiration. You might just discover that you are crazy for lavender and that you have an affinity for animal prints. Bring that storyline to life with your decor.

liner notes

Use painter's tape to create whimsical paint treatments—whether on a wall, a floor, or furnishings. Pro tip: Use a credit card's edge to rub the tape onto your desired surface. This technique secures the tape's seal, keeping paint from seeping beneath the tape edge and marring your crisp line. Here, we taped out a bold stripe pattern under a chair rail to give the mint-green wall extra dimension and fun. Plus, it's super easy and fast. We love a good chic DIY project.

shower power

Who says that shower curtains have to open from left to right or vice versa? That was rhetorical. We suggest draping an old tub as you would your windows—complete with a valance—to give your bathing experience a splash of brilliance.

WHY DON'T YOU

TAKE A TIRED SOFA WITH GOOD
bones and lavish it with big-time love. A jacked-up,
bold pattern (like the floral chintz here) provides a
contemporary spin that will bring a piece like this vintage
rolled-arm family heirloom crashing back to life.
The Madcaps almost cry when we see a great sofa sitting
curbside, and we try to rescue these lost souls whenever
we have the Subaru and some rope. Yes, that was
us on New York City's Fourteenth Street last weekend.

YOU OUGHT TO KNOW
SISTER PARISH

THE MADCAPS BOW DOWN TO THE
photographs of Sister Parish's Maine escape, the
Summer House, from back in the day (middle). If
you are like us, you will want to pin an image of her
Isleboro living room over your desk, to remind you that
too much pattern is sometimes not enough. (She even
inspired one of our fabrics. Well, there you have it!)
Parish, née Dorothy May Kinnicutt, took her upper-
crust upbringing and channeled it into interiors that
sang with American chic and traditional underpinnings
(see her designs for the Kennedy White House, top
and bottom). In many ways, Parish was to America what
Nancy Lancaster was to England, helping to define the
"country house" look that pairs the antique with the
new, tempered with a lived-in sensibility. Let's define
a few of the tenets of a Sister Parish room: Elaborately
painted or stained floors; Anglo-French furnishings;
heaps of chintz; bold colors; hooked rugs; needlepoint
pillows; and the list goes on from there. As the equally
renowned Albert Hadley, Parish's partner in Parish-
Hadley, said, her style was "freewheeling." Still, in
1974, *Vogue* championed her as "the most famous of all
living American women interior designers whose ideas
have influenced life-styles all over America." Noted
Parish, "Some think a decorator should change a house.
I try to give permanence to a house, to bring out the
experiences, the memories, the feelings that make it a
home." PS Dorothy Draper was Sister Parish's cousin!

Use PATTERN to make your space feel UNIQUE and SPECIAL.

Pattern is MODERN

Sometimes, life imitates ART,
or vice versa. When you want to
TRANSFORM a late 1990s-era
suburban home into something
with a little more PIZZAZZ—
and something that most certainly
doesn't look like your neighbors'
INTERIORS—be ready to take
a few design RISKS.

Pattern can turn that fantasy into your everyday reality.

INSPIRED BY MODERN, CUTTING-EDGE artwork, we wanted to bring a slice of urban living to this not-quite-country, two-story suburban home. Color was key to our vision, and we knew pattern would play a big part in creating architectural and visual interest where none existed before. Think stripes, color blocking, texture, and unexpected metallics.

The new-build home is transformed into something special with a carefully curated collection. Artwork by both up-and-comers and well-known artists fills larger walls and pass-through spaces, providing color and pattern. An oversize, Technicolor-hued painting is the centerpiece of the family room and hangs above a sculpture by Jonathan Seliger. In the foyer, a large signature flower by Michael De Feo adds a jolt of color. There's also a clever collage that mashes up the iconic Louis Vuitton logo and a piece with a blinking neon chicken. Really.

The dining room is wrapped in a silver-foil birch wallpaper and illuminated by a Tom Dixon pendant light (a nod to a vintage Absolut Vodka advertisement that starred model Rachel Williams in a Mylar minidress); the living room pairs bold pops of color—a bright red love seat with a yellow sofa and hot-pink curtain panels—with a splash of *Mad Men* mid century whimsy; and dramatic chocolate-and-white stripes give presence to a foyer and staircase that formerly lacked aplomb. Upstairs, the master bedroom pairs gray flannel with bold silk stripes and, again, is a study in unexpected color blocking and texture pairing. A faux fur rug adds to the unexpected storyline and softens the menswear-inspired gray hues.

Want your home to stand out from its neighbors? Why not give it a modernist frame of mind? You don't need to own a priceless collection. Look to eye-popping art by contemporary artists such as Joan Miró, Piet Mondrian, Jasper Johns, Andy Warhol, and others for inspiration, then bust out the paintbrush and have some fun. Bring in bold graphic patterns (e.g., color blocking or wide stripes), primary colors anchored with white and black, and a sprinkling of metallics for a bit of sparkle. Interior design is all about making your interior anything you want it to be, and pattern can turn that fantasy into your everyday reality.

The collection of eye-popping art and bold graphic pattern makes you question whether the bag of ice under Plexiglas in the family room is artwork, too, like the aluminum foil "boombox" by artist Jean Lowe in the master bedroom.

Carry pattern from room to room. In this home, the metallics and metals in the living room spill over into the dining room. Rich chocolate browns segue from the foyer into the living room.

opposite Set the scene with pattern—in other words, make a grand entrance. Striped wallpaper gives the double-height foyer a graphic tone (like a large art installation) and helps mask the foyer's many odd angles while adding drama and depth to the space where none existed previously. The zebra rug is another organic form of the stripe. You do not want to make everything too perfect or too linear, as that will have less impact.

left When we began overhauling their space, the owners' one caveat was that nothing should detract from the art. Thus our challenge: how to mix pattern without taking away from the collection of prints, paintings, and mixed media. Our solution was to use pattern in a more graphic way: Blocks of color—strong pink (the draperies), sunny yellow (the sofa), silver (the coffee table and rug), and rich chocolate brown (the cabinet)—draw attention around the room.

above Look for patterned accessories, such as this overscale light-up Buddha sculpture in rich orange, a color bridge between the room's reds and pinks. The pattern can be textural, such as the Buddha's headdress and ceremonial garb.

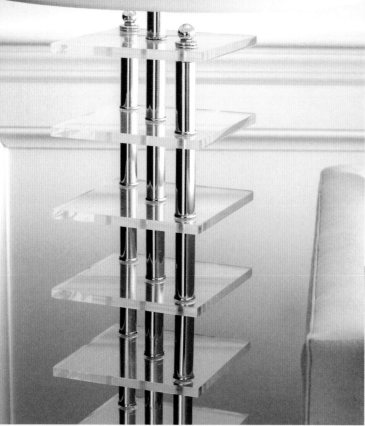

Why be afraid of color? You only live once, so don't settle for boring and expected.

above Details matter, such as the architectural Lucite-crafted base of this vintage lamp with its strong horizontal and vertical motifs.

right Patterned pillows are an easy way to dress up a solid sofa. Here, we selected a brown fretwork pattern to play off the yellow tufted sofa and echo the shape of the nearby floorlamp base.

opposite A bold hide-skin rug with silver accents adds some fun and unexpected whimsy to the linear arrangement of furniture. The red of the loveseat plays off the pink curtain panels and creates a hue-driven frisson and friction of color. The walls are glazed with a tonal stripe to tie back to the foyer. Artwork by the homeowners' children adds pops of color, as does the contemporary take on the needlepoint pillow.

A little sparkle—silvered wallpaper, lacquer, or mirrored surfaces—will transform any home into a glamorous getaway.

opposite & above A silvered forest of birch trees invites guests into the sparkling dining room. A spare Parsons-style dining table and bench, Lucite chairs, and a mirrored Tom Dixon chandelier complete the fun, modern look. Wrapping a room in a strong graphic pattern gives the space instant drama and flair without having to break down walls. The tree pattern is an organic version of the bold stripes in the foyer.

right Have some fun with your accessories, and keep your eyes open for treasures to layer into the mix. Here, a whimsical, white-on-white bust that hails from a department store prop sale mixes with a silvered coral candleholder. A single yellow orchid is a modern spin on the traditional floral arrangement.

this page In the family room, a nine-foot-long
canvas sets the tone. The painting's dimensions help
make the room feel more intimate. The furnishings
take design cues from the painting: The sofas
are large and linear and each is upholstered in a
different shade of blue. The lamps add symmetry
while bringing in additional colors from the art.

Rev up a cool, classic color such as gray with a brighter hue—perhaps a lemon-kissed yellow or just-plucked orange.

this page Color blocking is one of the design tools used to unify this suburban home's many rooms. In the master bedroom, a bright white ceiling and brilliantly lacquered white floor balance dark walls. Similarly, the chest of drawers visually balances the king-size bed. The bench at the foot of the bed adds a splash of brilliant color.

Don't take a room too seriously; add unexpected elements that will bring a smile—even on a Monday morning.

opposite Continuity of hue keeps this home feeling crisp and concise. Gray walls and the zigzag motif that zips across the armchair fabric continue two themes—stripes and blocks of bold color—also found throughout. Mirrors and chrome make an appearance, too, alongside eye-popping art, like the "boombox" sculpture by artist Jean Lowe.

left Modern pattern is simple and chic, like the shiny nailhead trim on this gray flannel headboard.

above Mirrored cabinets reflect both pattern and light, to lend almost neutral space to tight quarters.

PROJECT
STATE OF THE ART

ART IS A FANTASTIC WAY TO BRING PATTERN TO your walls quickly and easily. Think about pulling together mixed-media pieces from around the house and arranging them in a fun grouping with different shapes and sizes. Then start collecting new pieces, from vintage finds discovered at flea markets to modern pieces by up-and-comers. Who says that a contemporary home has to be spare and museum-like? Or that a traditional home has to be stuffy and old-fashioned? Certainly not the Madcap Cottage gents! Use modern art to bring pattern, color, and a lighthearted outlook into your home—no uncomfortable or precious anything allowed.

Here, a massive high-octane painting with heaps of pattern creates a focal point in the family room, thereby giving the double-height space an intimacy that was lacking. Note how the ottoman and decorative pillows pull colors from the painting. This treatment spills through the rest of the room—and then into the rest of the home.

Vintage prints collected in flea markets over the years march up and down the wall of a stairway and make a true statement thanks to their colorful mats and mismatched frames. With this artful arrangement in place, the mint-green backdrop now boasts a spirited dash of pattern and whimsy that gives this pass-through space panache.

An assortment of vintage botanical prints picked up in England punctuates a soothing blue wall in a dining room. Consistent mat treatments and frames bring the various florals together as a cohesive group.

In a tiny foyer, a floral-patterned chinoiserie wallpaper from Laura Ashley sets the scene. And, yes, you *can* hang artwork over a graphic wallpaper, friends! Here, antique botanical prints collected from travels work beautifully against the tree peonies and chirping birds. Have fun with your mat and frame treatments so that the artwork really stands out.

bonus idea

BUST OUT! The Madcaps love a good bust or sculpture placed upon a shelf or mantel—they add instant history, and you can dress them up. Keep your eyes open at flea markets and estate sales for all busts. We call this little filly Aunt Marge, and she is always decked out in an antique boater hat and ready for a little action.

TRADE SECRETS

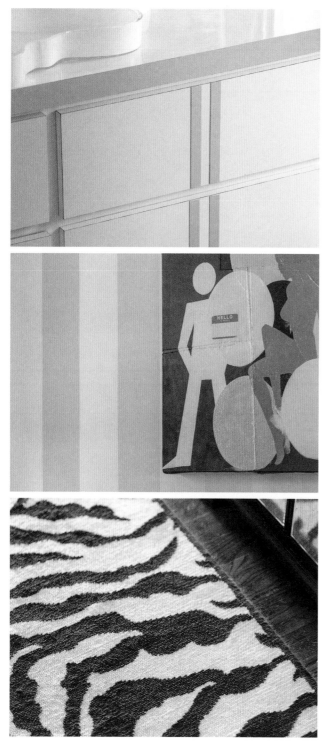

white knight

Egad, you say, the Madcap Cottage gents are a bit vanilla?! Yes, friends, we love white. Just remember that it *is* a hue, and there is a lot of variation between the different colorways. We once designed a room that had about twenty-two different shades of white in it, and the space was magical and gloriously patterned. Here, a vintage Pierre Cardin buffet purchased at auction boasts an ice-white body coat paired with a gray-white stripe to illuminate the details, and the result is dramatic, contemporary, and chic.

stripe tease

In the living room, we layered in pattern by glazing the walls in bold vertical stripes to give dimension to what was once seemingly acres of matte white. Plus, the glaze adds shine and a touch of sparkle, a theme that resonates throughout the house. Don't overlook decorative paint treatments when it comes to bringing pattern home. Subtle striation can be contemporary and exceptionally chic.

call of the wild

Animal prints are a design-world staple and work anywhere—literally, anywhere. The Madcaps believe that you should have at least one animal print in every room—just like lattice-patterned anything is heaven and auction houses are the stuff of dreams. Animal prints work equally wonderfully in contemporary spaces and traditional homes, and we love how the rich chocolate-brown zebra stripes on this area rug play off the stripes on the foyer's wallpaper.

gray's anatomy

We used a classic drapery treatment, including a box valance, on the windows in the master bedroom. What makes the window coverings look so modern and fresh is the rich color blocking on the panels and the juxtaposition of gray felt with cool gray silk on the valance. Don't be afraid to mix textiles to create bespoke brilliance: Here, the dialogue between the rich, lustrous silk and hard-wearing felt brings the yin and yang of masculine and feminine together beautifully.

WHY DON'T YOU

COLLECT MIXED-MEDIA PIECES THAT

make you smile and that don't only hang upon walls.
Art doesn't have to be fancy and highfalutin. Here, a smiley
face objet purchased at an art show takes center stage
upon a coffee table and offers a dash of whimsy as well as a
certain fumoir-fabulous quality—not that anyone smokes
indoors anymore, n'est-ce pas? The handblown glass
sculptures add further glamour. And the sculptural marbles
game set lends a spirit of playfulness and fun: No
home is complete without heaps of board games and
other options for indoor sport.

> "*Good design is in no way dependent on money. I like to spend the minimum of money and yet gain the maximum effect.*"
> —DAVID HICKS

YOU OUGHT TO KNOW
DAVID HICKS

IN OUR NEXT LIFE, THE MADCAPS HOPE to return as India Hicks, the model, entrepreneur, and überchic Harbour Island, Bahamas, denizen. Actually, we want to come back as Edwina Mountbatten, the last vicereine of India. Wait, maybe we want to be dashing Ashley Hicks and his fabulous wife, who wears bunny ears while scampering about the English countryside. Of course, all of these roads lead to the amazing David Hicks, father of India and Ashley and son-in-law of the aforementioned Countess Mountbatten—the kingpin of London postwar design and a gent who truly made the British capital swing. The Madcaps adore David Hicks's bold look-at-me use of color (bottom) and glorious geometrics (middle) that was anything but staid and still. Think eclectic to the max, whether in his interior design confections or in furnishings, wallpapers, and fabrics. Hicks' commissions were equally eclectic and ranged from the guest rooms at the Hotel Okura Tokyo to a Palladian-style villa in Portugal and the British Steel offices in New York. Said the late Hicks, who passed away far too young, "My greatest contribution as an interior designer has been to show people how to use bold color mixtures, how to use patterned carpets, how to light rooms, and how to mix old with new." The Madcaps are also passionate about Hicks for his glorious country estate in Oxfordshire, the Grove, and his fluency with crafting luxe gardens peppered with follies and stunning plane trees.

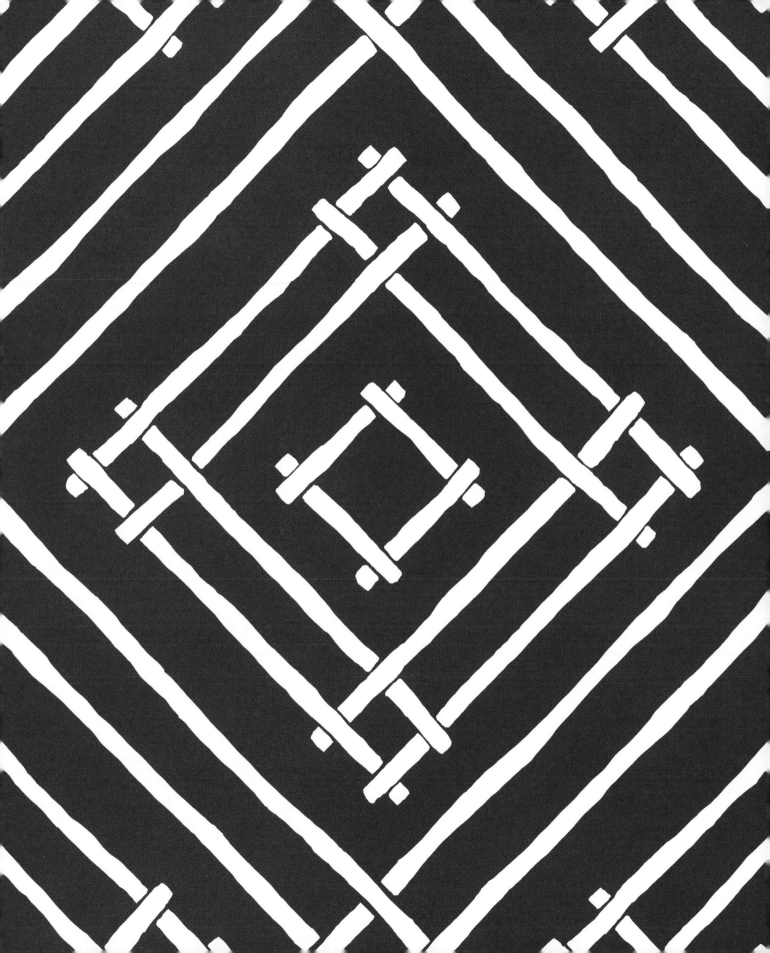

Layer, layer, LAYER *to create rooms that only get* BETTER *with* TIME *and where each piece tells a unique* STORY.

Pattern is ROMANTIC

WHO WOULDN'T be instantly
smitten with this 1840s-era former
SCHOOLHOUSE in upstate New York's
Catskill Mountains? The cottage-
like vibe, **VEST POCKET–SIZE** footprint,
and a location smack on the
Delaware River would sell even
the most hardened **NEW YORKER**.

THE DOWNSIDE? THE PLACE NEEDED
mountains of renovation—electrical, plumbing, the
works. The ultimate goal was to transform the eight-
hundred-square-foot space into a retreat for two. This
was not to be a place for houseguests, but rather a place
to read, relax, and escape from a hectic life. Visitors
could check into a charming inn nearby and come over
for dinner and Southsides, the house cocktail.

Today, the home is a relaxed, restful, and romantic
retreat where reading, gardening, cooking, and the
occasional gathering are the main activities.

Holding the place together are heaps and heaps
of florals and stripes and novelty prints that give the
cottage a personality far larger than its tiny footprint
would indicate. Every room is a conversation between
the indoors and the out thanks to the bold florals that
carry from the blossom-packed gardens to the window
panels, upholstered pieces, and wallcoverings. Even
the paint treatments within the cottage nod to the
great outdoors with the rich pinks, yellows, aquas, and
greens that serve as neutrals.

Thanks to the myriad pieces that were accumulated
over time, the cottage feels a tad like an English
country house—inviting, relaxed, and much loved.
The interior constantly evolves and changes.
New finds take the place of old, and furniture is
shuffled from room to room, layering in important
components so that rooms feel well lived in.

Bringing a splash of the romantic into your
own home is easy. Think blowsy florals paired with
stripes and other graphics. Find low-slung, shapely
furnishings that perfectly fit the scale of a room. Hit
the highway for antique finds, and browse flea markets
for eclectic vintage prints that you can frame. Pops of
unexpected colors add visual interest—and remember
that wallpaper helps alter a home's architecture by

A miniature foyer springs to life, ready for its close-up, thanks to a spirited mix of florals and marvelous moldings.

making a space appear much larger than it actually
is. And bringing the outdoors inside can create an
eternal-summer vibe year-round.

opposite Pattern goes all out in the cottage's cozy
(read: tiny!) entry. Thanks to a high-octane mix
of florals, graphics, and textures, the Madcaps
transformed what was once a narrow pass-through
into an inviting space that shouts "Welcome!"
Inspired by a journey to India, we layered summer-
kissed blossoms (the wallpaper), stripes (the
tongue-and-groove plank ceiling), and geometrics
(the bold Indian rug and pink paneling that nods to
a maharaja's palace). All of the colors in the space
spill over from the hues found in the exuberant
floral wallpaper.

If it works in nature, it will work in your living room.

opposite Bookcases are first and foremost utilitarian, but that does not mean they can't be visually inviting. This pink-hued fretwork affair adds both functionality and eye candy to the living room. The shelving's intricate lattice detailing references both the pattern of the room's wallpaper (albeit in a larger scale) and the designs found on the Indian rug in the foyer.

right Vibrant and unexpected colors and patterns flow from the foyer throughout this tiny house. The bold peacock-blue beams and casing define the home's living-cum-dining room. The color of the beams provides strong visual contrast to the subtle Gothic-inspired graphic paper. In total, the room encompasses about 300 square feet but feels much larger thanks to the boundary-blurring use of pattern.

this page Romantic pattern improves with layering. Here, in the petite low-ceilinged living-dining room (it's not quite eight feet), a kicky yellow peony-print fabric establishes the tone. The garden theme carries throughout the cozy space, with floral prints marching across every surface. Though it may seem counterintuitive to fill such a tiny home (it's just 800 square feet, total) with so much pattern and color, the reverse is actually true: The more going on in a small footprint, the less the walls feel as though they are closing in.

When layering patterns, look to a single hue that can connect an entire story.

left The living room's coffee table is a custom piece crafted from an antique Chinese coromandel screen panel. The table was selected to inject a hint of unexpected pattern into the room. Surprise and delight! That is the Madcap mantra.

above Don't forget to employ pattern upon casegood pieces, such as tables, china cabinets, and chests. The shelving unit in the living space, for instance, boasts a fretwork-lattice that offers a dynamic and airy quality instead of the typical rectangular bookshelf.

opposite When layering a variety of patterns on a piece of furniture, such as this sofa (or even in a room), look to one hue that can tie the storyline together. Here, shades of red, from coral to scarlet, connect the fabrics. Even a small dose of a hue—such as the reddish-pink bird-bedecked pillows—connects the patterns.

above Don't be afraid to mix styles and sensibilities in a room. Case in point, a kitchen that channels English, Venetian, and industrial influences to spirited effect. A whimsical and charming English paper anchors one wall in the kitchen and delivers a conversational focal point. The vintage QEII coronation sign brings a pop of color to the wall and references the colorways found on the antique Venetian lantern overhead. The concrete island nods to industrial chic and adds an urban spin to the cottage vibe.

right The big pattern statement in the kitchen: The mix of finishes paired with a limited color palette of blacks, grays, and pale blue. Natural materials, such as slate, marble, and wood, tell a textured and well-worn pattern story. The room's tongue-and-groove ceiling and chunky chiseled wood beams add visual interest on high. Although new, the finish on the custom cabinets was intentionally distressed to give the room a sense of history.

left Built as a schoolhouse in the mid-1800s, the cottage originally had no second floor. What is now the home's only bedroom came to be in the early 1900s, when extra living space was created by squeezing a floor just below the roofline. To make the low-ceilinged space function, the Madcaps filled in the area under the eaves with heaps of storage—bookcases on one side and cupboards on the other. The real pattern statement is the bed with its layers of mismatched linens and the boldly papered wall behind.

right Stumped on how to pair patterns? Select a common theme. Here, for instance, a peony blossom wallpaper lives in harmony with a rose-patterned lampshade. The commonality: Flowers in different scales.

Large-scale prints help visually expand a room's boundaries.

left Yellow and purple provide the room's predominant color themes and jump between the wallpaper, the matting on the framed art, and the high-gloss, built-in storage units. Note: Mismatched frames and a salon-style artwork arrangement give a small wall major oomph.

opposite One of the hallmarks of romantic pattern use is a bed layered in a mix of linens. Again, a common theme (here, a garden motif) holds the ensemble together—from geranium-patterned Euro pillow shams to peony-hued cases embroidered with a floral vine to a quilt inspired by mazes discovered at various romantic English country houses.

opposite The yellow and purple hues in the cozy den carry from the adjacent master bedroom and give the home's second floor a consistent color story. The colors hop nimbly between plaids, florals, and novelty prints to engaging effect. A small-scale armchair was never so visually stimulating!

right On the second-floor landing that leads to the bedroom, a multicolored striped runner serves as the bridge that connects the various floral prints. Stripes are the decorating world's unifying force. When you need to draw a connection between two prints and nothing seems to work, try a stripe and watch the magic happen.

PROJECT
DINING BY DESIGN

A COLORFUL, EYE-CATCHING TABLE SETTING IS
another way to invite pattern into your world quickly and without a major
investment of time or money. Why not pull out that wedding china or those
pieces that Granny left you that are just gathering dust in a hard-to-reach
cabinet above the refrigerator (you know, the shelves where you keep the
bread machine and the Crock-Pot)? Instead of sticking to your everyday
whites, have some fun with setting the table and use pattern to make a design
statement. Here, summer-kissed gingham napkins pair beautifully with
a floral tablecloth and place mats, ivy-wrapped chargers, and ruby-hued
drinking glasses. The patterned cachepot that holds peonies and carnations
finishes the look deliciously. Think of this tablescape as a very sophisticated
picnic—relaxed, easy, breezy, and bright.

Blues and whites set the stage
for a table that incorporates vintage
china that was rarely—if ever—used (we
removed circa-1962 Lord & Taylor price
tags). The mod floral place mats add
a contemporary twist and nod to the
blowsy hydrangeas tightly bunched in
the blue-and-white vase. The pale blue
napkins tie the visual knot.

Romance comes to the table in
the form of pale hues with delicate
florals on crisp white china and linens.
The scalloped and embroidered edges
on the napkins and place mats add
further elegance and set the scene for a
sublime summertime lunch. Complete
the look with pale pink roses.

Create the perfect table à deux.
A bold blue-and-white patterned place
mat adds drama to the faux bamboo—
inlaid table. Retro-patterned plates serve
up further visual comfort, and the dining
chair's cut-velvet upholstery only brings
further pattern élan to the equation.

bonus idea

Why not pick flowers from your garden and plunk them into a simple
water glass or clean-lined vase. Flower arranging need not be expensive
or fancy, as simple-chic is often the best solution. But let's say that
you are not the green-thumb type who cultivates flowers (such as the
peonies pictured here). Not to fret: Don't overlook the branches of a
particularly sculptural bush or tree, and grasses can be stunning when
artfully arranged. Houseplants are glorious, too. Plants and flowers can
take any space and make it magical. Bring the outdoors in, then watch
your interiors truly blossom.

TRADE SECRETS

paper dolls

eBay is a terrific source for vintage wallpaper, and we collect rolls not only to hang on our walls, but also as inspiration and for wrapping gifts and vintage screens. We also love to turn our throwback finds into bespoke lampshades finished off with trim. Two of our favorite lampshade makers are Elle Daniel in Sarasota, Florida, and Judy Lake, aka the Lampshade Lady, in Pawlet, Vermont. Both can make just about anything from paper and fabric (but not pleated pieces—that's a whole other conversation) and are social-media savvy.

think pink

Pink is our most favorite color—not bubblegum, but more the interior of a conch shell or a rich rosy pink, aka Fowler Pink (named for design force John Fowler of Colefax & Fowler; see our tribute to his partner, Nancy Lancaster, in Chapter 8). Here, we pulled two shades of pink from the Laura Ashley wallpaper and gave the cozy foyer a larger footprint through clever pattern and color play. And why not paint your front door a bright lemon yellow, and create further pattern by crafting faux paneling in an arch motif lifted from a maharaja's palace in Jaipur, India.

made in the shade

To carry the romantic vibe onto the window treatments in the kitchen, the Madcaps used a soft Roman shade instead of the typical hard-edged finish. The gathered style offers a certain relaxed luxe thanks to the generosity of the drape that perfectly mirrors the spirit of this cozy cottage.

granny chic

How did we ever start associating florals with Granny in a negative way? Frankly, we had a supercool grandmother who wore head-to-toe Pucci prints. Florals can be as contemporary as you want them to be, friends. Here, we mixed a clean-lined contemporary sofa with a midcentury-inspired chair and bold, bodacious blossoms in a far-reaching range of hues. It's romantic but never syrupy sweet. We would love to design an all-glass home, like that Philip Johnson landmark in Connecticut, in florals—it's all about a fun mix.

WHY DON'T YOU

HAVE SOME FUN WITH YOUR FURNISHINGS, and make them feel unique and individual. Dining tables and chairs can be so boring. Boring. Serious. Too done. Why not reupholster each of your dining chairs in a different fabric and watch your dinner guests gravitate to patterns that speak to them. Plus, it will help break the ice if, let's say, your husband's boss comes over and you have no clue what to talk about. "David, you can have the trellis in palm. And Maureen, please enjoy the fabulous floral in daffodil. More gin?"

LAURA ASHLEY

"I don't like ephemeral things; I like things that last forever."

—LAURA ASHLEY

MANY CHILDREN OF THE 1970S AND teenagers of the 1980s grew up in households that had head-to-toe Laura Ashley "moments" and rooms that boasted floral LA papers bolstered with LA white ginger-jar table lamps topped with LA pleated lampshades. Jason's Aunt Beth in Tallahassee even tied the knot in a Laura Ashley wedding dress that she scooped up in Oxford, England. A tip-to-toe lifestyle brand, genius! Laura Ashley was once so popular, retail outposts outfitted in patrician dark green stretched across the states, from Jason's Hyde Park neighborhood in Tampa, Florida, to John's hometown of Des Moines, Iowa. Although the brand isn't as prevalent as it once was, Laura Ashley's bodacious blossoms and vaguely chinoiserie patterns still pack a memorable punch. Thanks go to the Welsh-born Ashley for bringing a decidedly British vibe to the world: She began crafting headscarves in the 1950s before opening her first retail outpost in 1961. By 1975, the firm had more than forty shops and one thousand employees worldwide. Laura Ashley was a one-stop design shop before its time. "Really," Ashley noted, "I'm trying to keep things simple." Sadly, Laura Ashley passed away in 1985, and the firm never truly regained its balance. We still miss those incredible pleated lampshades, but Ashley's legacy remains, and her impact upon our design sensibility was massive.

MIX *masculine and feminine elements for a* ROOM *that is* CLUBBY-CHIC *and* DELICIOUSLY *comfortable.*

Pattern is
MASCULINE

ARE YOU AN inveterate traveler
with a city-slicker existence?
Do you crave the **TROPICAL** art-deco
vibe of destinations such as the iconic
Raleigh Hotel in Miami Beach?
That **TIMELESS** allure can be yours
when your interiors whisk you away
on far-flung **ADVENTURES**.

THIS SMALL ONE-BEDROOM apartment in New York City embodies a certain retro glamour (it is housed in a 1960s-era building designed by twentieth-century architect I. M. Pei), and its decor nods to an age when carefree insouciance trumped being tethered to our technology. Pattern is what imbues the home with a retro vibe—from dramatic leafy wallpapers and hand-painted bespoke furniture to rich cut velvets and fretwork motifs.

Miami Beach's Raleigh Hotel and art deco are a perennial inspiration, but we also set sail for Shanghai circa 1930 and infused some plucked-from-the-Bund brilliance (the Bund being Shanghai's corridor of historic art-deco edifices on the Huangpu River). What inspired the travel-minded trajectory? Wallpaper! Like you, we can't resist a swoon-worthy chinoiserie-style paper—especially for the living room.

Now, the building's beige-on-beige, anything-but-*Mad Men* public hallways lead you to the apartment's unassuming door. But once inside, a nightclub filled with rich woods, club chairs, skyscraper-inspired shelving, and Billie Holiday and Ella Fitzgerald crooning on the sound system reveals itself. A masculine color scheme of smoky grays, ebony, and brown wraps the apartment in richness and warmth. Much of this sensibility can be attributed to the pattern-rich wallpapers that anchor the various spaces—from the chinoiserie living room to the peony forest of a bedroom—and add instant architecture and visual appeal where white walls once glared menacingly. Think of patterned and textured wallpaper as a tool that can whisk you away to faraway places without the need for a passport and a travel budget. An abundance of natural light—a true oddity in New York City—and views of glittering rooftops keep the room from becoming a dark chasm. Bold cut-velvet geometrics envelop the living area's club-like swivel armchairs

Wrap a room in an exotic wallpaper, and you are transported to another era, no passing go.

and dining space's banquette. Use three-dimensional patterns to add layering to a space and give further visual depth and dimension. Mix in antiques and vintage finds to continue the storyline at hand. In the bedroom, we chose carved-wood Asian table lamps with custom grass-cloth shades to bookend a velvet-wrapped skyscraper-influenced headboard that's pure Hollywood. And we commissioned a custom hand-painted bookshelf that beautifully houses a collection of 1930s-to-midcentury memorabilia, including Stork Club ashtrays and gazelle-emblazoned cigarette boxes. Remember that sometimes going the custom route can be the best solution for a piece of furniture that will perfectly fit a space.

opposite You can create a masculine enclave inspired by the glamour of global travel with a rich color scheme, patterns, and furnishings inspired by a specific style (here, art deco) and a specific location and era (here, Shanghai in the 1930s).

*Dream,
envision, and
make magic
with pattern.*

this page Think clubby, chic, and sophisticated abstract patterns, moody colors, and deco-style chinoiserie, and voilà! Takeaway: Stumped on how to embrace pattern? Create a storyline for your home, and turn to pattern to make that dream a reality. Throwback Shanghai in Manhattan's East Thirties, why not!

Treat black as a neutral—and a foundation for various patterns in a room.

opposite Bold patterns define the cut-velvet fabrics used to cover the living room sofa and its accompanying cushions, including cherry blossoms and branches, abstract palm leaves, and a zigzag motif reminiscent of the top of the Chrysler Building.

left Look to auction houses and antiques stores for finds that will bring a room to life, such as this beautifully detailed torchiere floor lamp.

above Our client owned this vintage French metal laundry cart, but it was a sad army green and the cart, stuck in a closet, lacked purpose. The Madcaps rescued the little lady by having her powder coated a sleek black with a chic white stripe and then transformed the piece into a living room bar cart.

Delicious details add just the right amount of (unique) chic.

left Masculine pattern is all about the interplay between big, bold geometric statements, such as the two-tone emerald-and-black cut velvet on this dining chair seat, and the more subtle, such as the black-on-gray honeycomb rug.

opposite To give the light-filled apartment moody atmosphere, the Madcaps covered one wall in the living room with glamorous Asian-inspired wallpaper. The wall was just the starting point. Note how we carried the chinoiserie vibe throughout the room, from the brass pulls on the serving cabinet to the vintage gilded and lacquered faux bamboo dining table. Be sure to bring a storyline to fruition: You can dip a toe in the water, but if you want the complete pattern effect, go full force by bringing fabrics and accessories into the mix.

left Artwork need not be a painting or a print. The Madcaps found this antique French deco needlepoint tapestry at an auction and snapped it up. Framed and floating in a streamlined gilded wood case, the tapestry now anchors the wall over the dining nook banquette. Notice how the channel-back banquette speaks to the shape of the skyscraper-like headboard in the apartment's bedroom. It's all about carrying a storyline between rooms.

right In the dining nook—a corner of the living room outfitted with a custom banquette and a vintage table and chairs—visitors are whisked away to the Bund district of 1930s-era Shanghai. Thank dappled chinoiserie wallpaper, luxe jewel-toned velvet upholstery, and the rich, gleaming wood grain of art deco period furnishings for capturing this transporting sensibility.

this page Shape and pattern carry the glamorous Shanghai vibe from the living room into the master bedroom. A skyline-shaped deco-style upholstered bed, with its rich, silky velvet fabric, exudes 1930s glamour. A floral but decidedly masculine peony-tree-emblazoned wallpaper wraps the space, lending just the right amount of oriental drama to the design scheme. A carefully curated mix of antique art deco furnishings—like the wood-framed armchair in the corner—completes the look, lending an air of period authenticity.

PROJECT
PAINT THE TOWN

IF YOU ARE LIKE US, YOU ARE PASSIONATE ABOUT
furnishings that tell a story and go mad for painted details on furniture. So
you will understand why we could not resist designing this bespoke bookshelf
with heaps of details, including cocktail trays that slide out (fabulous, right?).
John sketched all of the gazelles that leap to and fro. The black exterior frames
the aqua interior so that the shelves truly stand out, and punched-out silver
medallions flank the base to deliver pattern from the ground up. Your mission,
should you choose to accept it: Take a piece of furniture from a flea market or
yard sale and give it a spirited decorative paint treatment. You might even be
surprised by how much fun you have bringing your creative vision to life.

1

2

3

Look for pattern upon furnishings: This dining table has gold-leafed faux-bamboo edges, a black lacquer band, and a rich wood top with an embossed scene. Now that's real pattern punch!

An antique chinoiserie cabinet, rich with hand-painted fretwork and garden-themed details, serves as the perfect bar. The oxblood red-and-black cabinet stands out against the Gothic English wallpaper and makes a bold statement. Keep your eyes open at vintage stores and flea markets for statement-making furnishings that can create focal points.

The table is truly a focal point in the Chinese-inspired living room (see Chapter 8) and adds yet another unexpected pattern in a decidedly sophisticated environment. Eglomise, or reverse-painted glass, is a stunning decorative treatment, so, of course, dear readers, you know that we couldn't pass up purchasing this antique mirrored coffee table with its gracefully tapered legs, floral eglomise detailing, and scalloped edges.

bonus idea

Details are all-important in an interiors scheme. It might be a patterned decorative pillow that lends extra oomph to a sofa or armchair, or a striped throw that adds a sense of cozy chic. Or go all out with bespoke details! This custom-crafted bookshelf has pullout trays hand painted with monkeys scampering about with cocktail glasses, the perfect perches for Negronis and Manhattans—neat, natch. The trays are hidden inside the bookshelf (at left) most of the time, but when they are used, the naughty monkeys always bring a smile. And that's truly what decor should do—make you smile.

TRADE SECRETS

one of a kind

No room is complete without a piece or two of vintage furniture or antique accessories. Here we sourced an antique art deco armchair to perfectly fit a corner in the master bedroom and help convey the Shanghai 1930s storyline. Turn to local antiques stores and flea markets for finds that can be restored or reupholstered, and don't overlook online sources, too. We believe in investing in furnishings with a provenance when the situation is appropriate. In this space, the chair is truly icing on the cake.

all about accessories

As Clairee Belcher sagely suggested in the film *Steel Magnolias*, "The only thing that separates us from the animals is our ability to accessorize." Don't you agree? It's all about layering and bringing provenance and stories to life. Start collecting on your travels, visit flea markets, hit up consignment shops, and peruse the aisles of your favorite secondhand store. Get to collecting, and then layer these pieces into your space, letting them shine anew.

fabric of life

Use fabric to bring your home-environment manifesto to life. Here, a clubby, art deco–driven apartment nods to Miami and its historic art deco architecture, so the Madcaps used rich textiles for cinematic splendor. Cut velvets in palm-leaf patterns play against a cool-blue woven upholstery. Clubby, check. Deco, yes. Miami, absolutely. Patterns save the day once again.

dark and lovely

Using black as a design staple is a great trick of the trade. Often overlooked as too severe or overpowering, black can actually help you anchor a space. Take this bedroom, where the matte-black chinoiserie-patterned wallpaper with its peony trees pairs wonderfully with the high-gloss painted door and closet in the background and adds further dimension to the polished-wood bookcase (custom-designed and based on an original spotted at the iconic Raleigh Hotel in Miami Beach).

WHY DON'T YOU

START A COLLECTION—AND WE
don't mean stamps and coins. Collect art,
paperweights, art deco-era Bakelite boxes, vintage
tobacciana (tobacco products, such as match
strikes)—really anything . . . just not commemorative
spoons. It's all about the layering, folks. And
bringing your personal storyline to life through objects
and items that really speak to you, of course.

"Great blends of pattern, like great dishes, must be carefully tasted. And constant tasting is what teaches a cook how to taste."

—BILLY BALDWIN

YOU OUGHT TO KNOW
BILLY BALDWIN

NO, DEAR READER, BILLY BALDWIN is NOT one of Alec's brothers. Rather, this iconic—but not-much-mentioned—design force had a profound impact on late twentieth-century American interior decoration. He preferred the unfussy to the jumbled and the chaotic—and was a fan of employing simple cottons, geometrics, and natural fibers such as rattan and bamboo. Color was also a key tenet of his design repertoire (top). Noted Baldwin, "I suppose one could say that I almost started the vogue for a clear, Matisse-like decorating palette" (middle). Standout projects included Diana Vreeland's fabled Park Avenue living room (aka, the red-on-red "garden in hell"), the sumptuous Kenneth hair salon in New York City (bottom), and myriad homes for Jackie Onassis stretching from Virginia to the Greek isles. A native of Baltimore, Baldwin honed his skills under the also oft-forgotten Ruby Ross Wood in New York City before branching out on his own and crafting pure magic. Baldwin tended to use one signature pattern in a room and pull colors from that throughout a space. He had a very graphic sensibility. His rooms are terrifically timeless and hold true now in the photographs just as they did when they were originally crafted decades ago.

Have FUN with your INTERIORS. (If you want to live in a museum, sneak into The Met AFTER HOURS.)

Pattern is PLAYFUL

A **COVERED PORCH** is a perfect blend
of indoors and out, of work and play,
of **PURPOSE** and party. And when
a tiny weekend **COTTAGE** is in need
of entertaining space, a **SCREENED**
room allows for extra square footage
on the best days of the year.

AT ONE COTTAGE SMACK IN THE
heart of New York's bucolic Catskill Mountains, we
fixed our eyes firmly on the detached former garage.
The pragmatic advice was to, "Tear it down," and
there were plenty of reasons to comply: the wonky
roof; the tacked-on addition crafted of, seemingly,
glue and particleboard; and the floor that was almost
nonexistent, for a few. Plenty of mouse droppings,
a buzzing hornets' nest, and a large hole in the roof
patched with a blue tarp affixed by staples almost made
us acquiesce.

But visions of an outdoor space that could
morph from dinner party spot to living room to the
occasional screened-in sleeping porch helped us
overlook the structure's shortcomings.

After propping up the roof, cementing the floor,
adding some screens, and giving it a lick of paint (and
saying sayonara to Mr. Hornet and his buzzy pals), we
set to work adding heaps of color and pattern.

We trawled flea markets and jumble sales for
seating, side tables, and vintage rattan furniture
to marry the comfort of indoors with outdoor
sensibilities. Outdoor fabrics, chosen for their jolts
of color and strong patterns, enlivened the space. We
picked up an outdoor rug and unearthed a pair of
pagoda-style lanterns to dangle overhead, offering a
taste of the Royal Pavilion in Brighton, England.

With the ceiling doused in a pale blue hue, as a
nod to the traditional Southern porch, and floral
curtain panels hung over the newly installed screens,
the Pavilion came together as a riot of embellishment
and color. It is now a space where gatherings turn into
parties and guests never want to leave.

Creating your own alfresco space is easy with our
recipe: First, roof or no roof, bring in overhead
interest with inexpensive paper lanterns, bunting,
and string lights. Then add comfortable outdoor

There are no rules here, friends. Mix whatever feels right and have some fun.

furnishings (no need to spend your savings—just grab
found pieces and hand-me-downs and give them
a fresh coat of spray paint) and plump them up with
cushions, pillows, and throws in bright colors and
patterns. Next, cover a not-so-pretty floor with paint
and a kicky indoor-outdoor rug. And finally, add
friends, music, nibbles, and cocktails, and let the
party begin!

If you are pattern shy, why not test the waters with
a temporary space, perhaps a porch or a garden retreat.
There are no rules here, friends. Mix whatever feels
right and have some fun. If you want to bring pattern
home in a small way, also think about refreshers:
Switch out the throw pillows on a sofa, or replace
your curtains. But if you have a porch, why not give
it an overhaul that will have the neighbors clamoring
to come over for cocktails. Anything goes—the space
is temporary!

opposite Welcome to the Little House, a former
garage that dates from the 1920s and that has been
repurposed as a screened-in outdoor living room
or summerhouse. The vintage sign from which the
building takes its name was unearthed at a yard sale.
Step inside, and embrace the pattern-packed fun!

this page Why not try mixing patterns in a seasonal space, perhaps a casual porch or garden retreat. In this former garage, the Madcaps painted the walls white and the ceiling blue and filled the space with vintage white rattan. All of the white helps ground the heaps of mismatched vibrant patterns. Think garden party, and pour the cocktails.

right Layer in pillows that are fun and whimsical and anything but boring. Here, the Madcaps used an embroidered floral cotton to create luxe pillows that play perfectly with the chair's monkey-and-palm cushions. Green is the tie that binds the two patterns together. The yellow welting adds an unexpected kick.

opposite A soft blue paint gives the rustic wood ceiling a light and airy look. The texture of the wood siding complements the slatted pattern of the wicker chairs. The rattan hood-style beach chair and layers of bunting and lanterns help to visually bring the peaked ceiling down to a more intimate scale.

opposite The Madcap gents love recycling vintage finds into stylish, useful conversation starters with a purpose. Case in point: We took a vintage Red Dot potato chips canister that we discovered at a local flea market and turned it into a table lamp with the help of a lighting kit (available at any hardware store or online) and a sharp black paper shade. A kicky floral pillow with a painterly flange adds further fun.

right A vivid zigzag-patterned indoor-outdoor rug brings a bold design statement to the porch's rustic floor and anchors a whimsical faux-bois cement garden bench. The blue of the rug picks up the similar hue that wraps the ceiling.

PROJECT
PARTY TIME

THERE'S NOTHING LIKE COLORFUL, PATTERN- bedecked lanterns to evoke a spirit of fun and the sense that scintillating shenanigans are about to commence. We love the word *shenanigans*, don't you? In this summer house, inexpensive Chinese lanterns hang from fishing wire, and the colorful tasseled creations shimmy and shake in the balmy summer breezes. The large, round lanterns contain flameless LED votive candles and cast marvelous shadows as the sun sets. Crank up the color-packed lanterns, then kick up your heels and watch the party take flight.

Vintage wallpaper that mimics
the room's cut-velvet leaf-pattern
upholstery dresses custom lampshades
at this Manhattan aerie (Chapter 5).
Lampshades are a great place to invest
in custom handiwork. If you are
crafty, you can learn to make shades
yourself, but we like to leave it to the
pros. The shade here is the perfect
accompaniment to the vintage art-
deco base, and the pattern plays
wonderfully with the scenic wallpaper.

An opaque chocolate-brown shade
atop a chinoiserie table lamp shows
off its patterned inner lining when
the light is turned on: Flip the switch
and rich florals immediately bloom
in the forefront. We love the idea that
pattern can be turned on and off. With
that said, these drum shades feature
shantung silk exteriors, so they still have
a wonderful texture that adds dimension
whether lit or unlit. The shades hail
from Anthropologie, a great source for
lampshades with unique underpinnings.

A rich, timeless floral pattern takes
center stage on a tapered shade in this
elegant master bedroom. Add a splash of
brushed fringe, and the mix is magical.
Don't forget exceptional details: While
the pale blue gourd lamp would have been
lovely with a neutral lampshade, the floral
topper makes it simply marvelous.

bonus idea

Line your lampshades with a metallic finish to cast a soft, warm glow,
rather than that awful harsh light courtesy of today's LED bulbs, an
invention of the devil himself! In this peaceful Manhattan apartment,
the light from the silvery lampshade helps soften the hard-edged,
industrial lines of exposed brick walls and a stone-topped console.

TRADE SECRETS

just picked

When you are shopping at flea markets and garage sales, keep an eye out for unusual containers that you can repurpose as vases. This vintage cookie jar is a fun, unexpected way to display flowers cut fresh from the garden and it adds just the right amount of whimsy.

weave around

Vintage rattan gets our hearts racing. Plus, you can often find it for a great price at flea markets and consignment shops. Rattan offers that quality of a mini vacation, sort of like wine in a box. Oh, did we say that? Try taking some vintage rattan (as we did from our family's former beach house) and having it painted by a local craftsman in a spray booth—or spray paint it yourself in the backyard on a wind-free day. Playful, effervescent cushions in a bold tropical woven fabric add just the right amount of breezy chic to the storyline.

mix, don't match

Take your curtains and make them sensational, courtesy of multiple patterns, such as the floral-loves-gingham pair here. Pink is the color thread that connects the two patterns: The graphic adds a charming, country-style contrast to the climbing roses that scamper about in full bloom. And who says your rug has to match your drapes? Oh, that's another story. We meant: Who says that your curtain rods have to match your curtain rings? We certainly didn't. Here, off-the-rack painted rods and wood rings from Smith & Noble have been given a bespoke treatment by not being matchy-matchy.

green with envy

An assortment of geraniums and other potted plants carries the porch's floral theme from the drapery panels and pillows to an antique wicker table in an easy, breezy fashion. Don't you love to bring the great outdoors in, creating an indoor-outdoor dialogue? (And plants always add warmth and a lived-in quality to a home.) If you aren't great with plants, try a hard-to-kill ivy or fern.

WHY DON'T YOU

HAVE FUN WITH YOUR BAR ACCESSORIES!
Here, a laminate floral serving tray and whimsical
bar accoutrements invite guests to partake in cocktails
and linger longer. The tray's bold floral print references the
porch's bloom-bedecked houseplants and fabrics. We love
the scampish simian bottle opener, even though he tends
to swipe the bar snacks when no one is looking. Naughty monkey!

"I have no time for boring furniture, boring fabrics, or boring people."

—ROSE CUMMING

YOU OUGHT TO KNOW
ROSE CUMMING

AUSTRALIAN-GONE-AMERICAN DESIGN force Rose Cumming's magical fabrics are swoonworthy, and happily still in production courtesy of the Dessin Fournir Companies. Think iconic leopard spots and tropical leaves seemingly dipped into paint then pressed against fabric. Born to English parents and raised on an Australian sheep ranch, Cumming landed on the US shores in 1917. A fantastic colorist, Cumming once proclaimed, "Parrots are blue and green. Why shouldn't fabrics be?" She found inspiration among far-flung decades and reference points—channeling Mylar-wrapped walls as ably as she did a spirited dash of Victoriana (top) or eighteenth century French antiques. Cumming loved chinoiserie, invented metallic wallpaper, and was a fan of lacquered walls and smoky mirrors (below). Her Midtown Manhattan townhouse, with its Tiffany-blue music room and drawing room with walls covered in an eighteenth century chinoiserie paper (middle), was known for its ecclectic mix of furnishings and its exuberant color story. Her personal style was equally eclectic and intriguing: She was known for her purple hair and overblown hats as much as for her razor-sharp wit and outspokenness. Or as Cumming said, "I have no time for boring furniture, boring fabrics, or boring people." Don't you agree? Life is short, why settle for the banal?

Create a DIALOGUE between the INDOORS and the out. Why not bring the COLORS of your GARDEN into the rooms of your house?

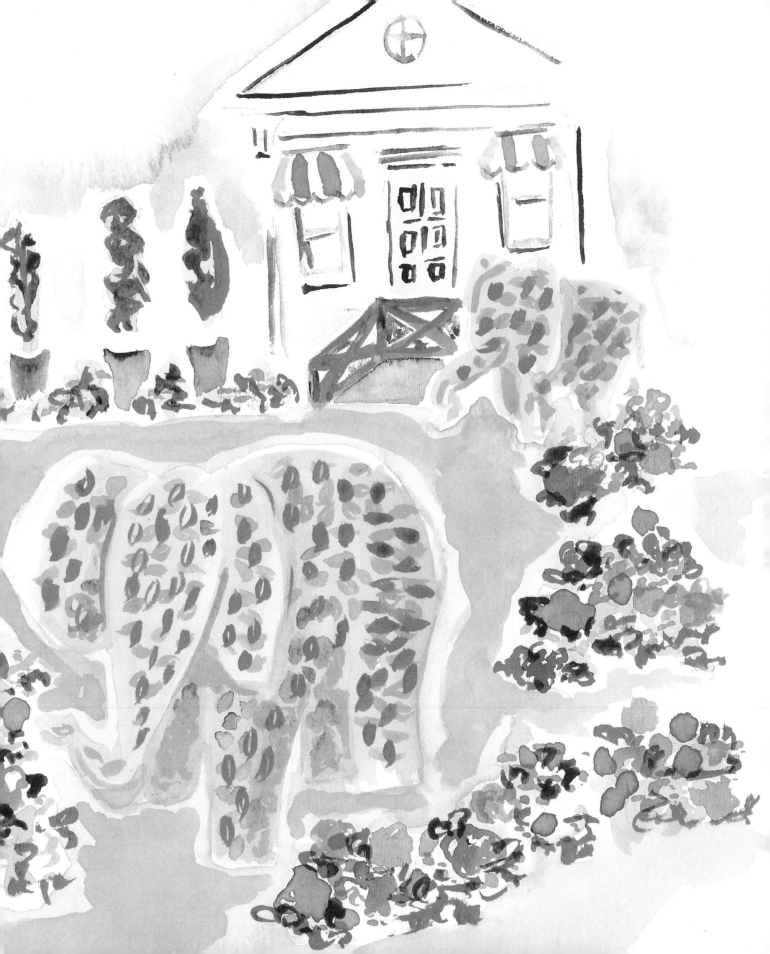

Pattern is PEACEFUL

DREAMING of a home that is a soothing,
cosseting OASIS, but your reality is a space
that doesn't quite come together?
Many apartment dwellers, especially those
who inhabit particularly UNUSUAL
layouts such as lofts (where traveling from
entry to living area can require strutting down
a sixty-foot-long runway of a hallway),
want to SHIFT FOCUS to their homes' more
appreciated architectural features.

Create a home that feels cool, calm, and collected with luxe textures and subtle patterns.

TO CREATE A ZEN-LIKE ESCAPE FROM the bustling city beyond, we placed the focus on luxury, glamour, and a soothing scheme of color and pattern—the perfect foils to the apartment's hard surfaces of concrete, stainless steel, and exposed brick. Silver, pale lavender, gold, and gray, rather than big, bold hues, pair with textured fabrics and finishes to make a soothing yet sparkling star turn. On the stairway wall, silk wallpaper with a wonderful shantung-style finish wraps the path to the bedroom. In the dining area, a sturdy concrete console table and brick wall meet their visual opposites in the custom sculptural mercury glass chandelier hanging high above a glass-and-wood dining table and chairs dressed in a winter-white shagreen-like fabric. The living area's fireplace wall is covered in what appears to be elegant silver tiles, but is actually a wallcovering that is a textural juxtaposition to the luxe velvet and silk upholstery fabrics on the sofa and chairs. Glistening polka dots dance across a silk area rug that tops high-gloss ebony wood floors. Rich accessories— from faux-fur throws to sumptuous silk pillows—are the gems that make this oasis glimmer and shine. In the loft bedroom, white lacquer pairs with carved-stone table lamps, and rich lavender velvets and custom bedding provide a soothing tonic to the angular spaces and cut-out architecture.

If glamour is a part of your decorating desire, use glints of silver and gold (yes, both!) alongside a subtle color palette; bring in barely there patterns on touchable fabrics and wallcoverings; balance rough textures (brick and concrete) with smooth (glass and silk). Don't forget the final flourishes that are the jewelry to your room's little black dress: fabulous lighting fixtures, plump pillows, and art. With a layer of soothing pattern on every surface, your reality will soon be the luxe oasis you crave.

Pattern can be peaceful, relaxing, and quiet. It can be subdued and understated. Remember, too, that pattern can be conveyed through the materials you select for your home—whether stone, mirror, cement, tile, or something else entirely.

opposite In every room of a home or apartment, the Madcaps like to introduce an element of surprise. Here, one such element is the gold lacquered side table that plays off the framed artwork beyond the sofa. The frosted glass wall that encloses the bathroom is practical, allowing natural light into what would otherwise be a dark space and creating a surface treatment that has more visual depth than a painted wall. To bring the glass wall into the overall look of the space, we enclosed the fireplace's fire box in mirrored tiles and papered the surface of the chimney in a lacquered, mirrorlike silver paper. The wall leading up the stairs carries the shimmering tones into the loft.

Make your home a peaceful sanctuary, away from the hustle and bustle of everyday life. Turn off social media for a spell, and take a deep breath.

this page It's important to think about pattern from all angles, especially in a space where a room will be viewed at eye level and also from high above. (Here, the living-dining room of a peaceful Manhattan apartment is viewed from the loft bedroom.) The rug's swirling dots echo the curved shape of the sofa. In the dining room, glass inserts in the wood-frame table allow the dining chairs' textured fabric seats to stand out. The white-painted brick wall, behind, brings an industrial element into the pattern mix.

opposite Peaceful pattern is all about a comfortable balance of solids and textures, lights and darks, and the occasional accent, such as the rose-colored silk draperies that frame the loft's soaring windows and add luxe texture beside the industrial, painted brick wall.

above The dining area's shimmery chandelier is a Madcap Cottage creation crafted by bringing together two different pendant lights—one made of silvery mercury glass and the other a crystal-clear teardrop.

right Pillows are an easy way to introduce powerful statement patterns into an otherwise peaceful design scheme. The patterns in question do not have to be prints but rather can be more textural in nature, such as embroidered motifs or faux animal skin. The colors of the pillows should blend with the rest of the colors in the space. Don't introduce another statement color or you will upset the peaceful balance. Instead, stay within the same color families: in this case grays, beiges, violets, and creamy whites.

right One of the few decorating rules you should never break: Always play to the architecture of a space. Here, to help humanize the soaring scale of the fireplace chimney breast, the Madcaps constructed an equally towering shelving unit. The shelving balances the height of the chimney and tricks the eye into seeing the soaring space at a different level.

opposite The apartment's bedroom owes its peaceful appearance to a muted color palette and subtle use of pattern. The silver-leaf finish of the custom Parsons-style night tables blends in quietly with both the upholstery on the bed and the paint on the wall. The lamp's stone base, though a mixture of mottled colors, pairs beautifully with the bedding.

this page In the loft bedroom, the walls and ceiling
are painted a shade of pale gray to contrast with the silk
wallcovering that lines the staircase wall opposite the bed.
The gray hue overhead (mapped out with a laser line for
a crisp, clean finish) visually masks the low ceiling height
and makes the space feel cozier than the voluminous
room it overlooks. Because the bedroom opens to the
living area below, all of the colors and textures relate
back to the room downstairs. For example, the fabric
on the upholstered bed frame is the same subtle striéd
cotton used to cover the living room chaise.

PROJECT
OFF THE WALL

IN A MANHATTAN APARTMENT, THE MADCAPS USED
multiple tiles on a fireplace surround, including stone subway tiles and
larger mirrored tiles, paired with sparkling silvery wallpaper. We love the
combination of organic stone with the silvery tiles that brings the room's
reflected patterns to life. Both tiles spill into a foil wallpaper that continues
the sparkle-tinged theme up the soaring fireplace to the ceiling high above.
Use wallpaper to highlight architecture and add visual interest where none
existed before. And tile, ooh-la-la! We all need to have more fun with tile
and treat it as more than a material for floors, bathrooms, and kitchens.

A vintage gilt sconce soaks in the sun against throwback wallpaper rich with peonies and other chinoiserie motifs. Mix in pleated lampshades with pom-pom detailing, and the pairing is pure magic. Layer in textures, trims, and details, dear readers, to make every moment in a room exceptional.

Classic lattice-pattern wallpaper is the perfect backdrop to garden-themed vintage artwork and lighting that brings the plucked-from-the-yard motif to life in three dimensions. Artwork is a wonderful way to bring pattern to life— not only through the artwork itself but courtesy of frames and matting, too.

Retro, 1930s-style wallpaper anchors a kitchen wall that lacked visual interest and serves as a welcoming beacon at the entrance to this cozy apartment. Go big and bold with a wallpaper when you have a wall that needs maximum impact.

bonus idea

GREEN WITH ENVY Find a unique wallpaper to give a wall in your home that extra élan. Here, the Madcap Cottage gents crafted a bespoke paper (it has our pound-rescue pups Jasper, Amy Petunia, and Weenie in it) in cahoots with our friends at Gracie Studio, but you can turn to eBay or flea markets to find wallpapers that capture your sensibility and are deliciously affordable, too. Throw in a chair with a bold pattern mix—such as florals with a lattice pattern—and the pairing is luxe and lovely and uniquely YOU.

TRADE SECRETS

vanity fair

Silvery surfaces take center stage on the apartment's soaring fireplace with its foil wallpaper combined with a round mirror. The combination of reflective surfaces—paired with the organic, burnished, hammered-metal mirror frame—adds dimension, texture, and drama to the room.

skin is in

Pattern can be subdued and spare: Take this shagreen-textured cotton-velvet fabric on the dining room chairs that captures the qualities of stingray skin. From a distance, the chairs' upholstery reads as all white against the dark wood frames; up close, however, the eye discerns the subtle and luxurious pattern that adds dimension and depth.

round and round

The shape of furniture is pattern, too. Here, a round coffee table with its linen-wrapped finish offers a soothing tonic and furthers the peaceful vibe without hard angles and straight lines. The round shape also plays off the circles that swim across the shimmery silk rug, carrying the pattern play from the floor up. The rounded glass accessories perched atop the table continue the design thread.

sheer luck

Pale, striated sheer shades cover the oversize windows in the living room and shield views of the hustle and bustle of Broadway far below. The faint pattern that wraps the iridescent shades can only be seen when the light hits them just so, adding a luxurious, almost-handspun quality to what could have been run-of-the-mill. Don't overlook the bespoke, pattern-driven details that elevate the usual to the exceptional.

WHY DON'T YOU

USE TEXTURE AS PATTERN, TOO
(especially fabulous faux-fur pillows or a throw). Our
pound-rescue posse is crazy about faux fur and
always hogs the covers when the throw materializes in late
fall. Speaking of which, why not switch out your
pillows and such on a seasonal basis to keep a room
feeling fresh? Layer in blankets as the temperature dips
and arrange cotton throw pillows come summer.

YOU OUGHT TO KNOW
SYRIE MAUGHAM

WHITE UPON WHITE UPON WHITE IS especially intriguing when you are known for layering prints upon prints upon prints. We like the idea of a neutral space in theory, but would the Madcaps ever want to live in such a room? We'd certainly spill red wine within a nanosecond, and the dogs would shed all over, and who has time to let Stanley Steemer in for constant cleanings? Still, the signature Syrie Maugham "look," a mix of Hollywood glamour splashed with heaps of mirrors, fur carpets, and white leather, tempts us. But maybe only in a fantasy world occupied by the likes of Jean Harlow (bottom). Thank the British design force of the 1920s and 1930s for crafting the first all-white room and for taking antiques and giving them a new look, the so-called "Maugham treatment," thanks to pickling and painting (top). Maugham's signature style eventually morphed into the realm of Baroque (middle) and the addition of bold colors—from shocking Schiaparelli pink to emerald greens and red. By all accounts, Maugham was something of a dictator—she was the inspiration for the social-climbing designer who renovates London townhomes in sheepskin and chrome in *A Handful of Dust*, penned by Evelyn Waugh—but her mark was indelible.

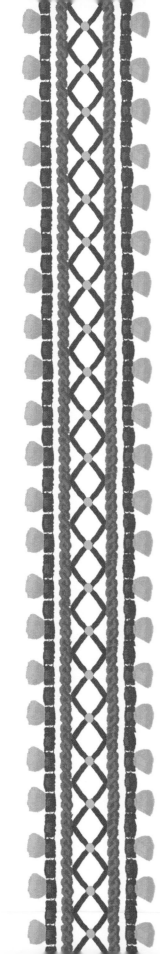
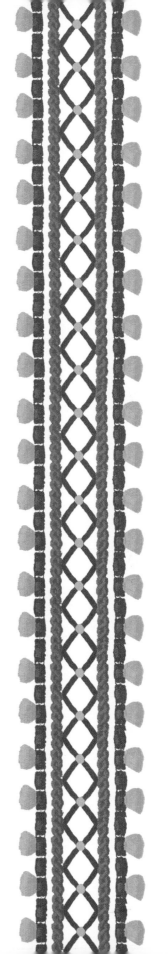

BEAUTIFUL and USEFUL should go hand in hand. If you can't PUT your FEET up, what's the point?

Pattern is SOPHISTICATED

WHEN YOU MAKE the leap to a house—
a real grown-up house like this 1930s-era
Regency-style white **BRICK** home—
why not give it some **MAGIC** to make it
sophisticated *and* utterly livable? We love
the idea of **CRAFTING** a home that is chic
yet relaxed. A place that unexpectedly
throws **CARE** to the wind.

Nod to the past, but always with a cheeky sense of humor.

AS INTERIOR DESIGNERS WITH roots as editors, we craft a mission statement for each home we renovate. Here, the mandate was to return the home to its 1930s-era origins. The goal was to create a sophisticated English country house where boozy Sunday lunches would be commonplace and a spirit of relaxed fun, and a certain *luxe, calme et volupté*, would pervade.

Fast forward . . .

The foyer, now lit up thanks to the removal of two closets and the addition of sidelights, sparkles with decorative paint wall treatments (a nod to British muralist Rex Whistler) that march up the main stairway and play off the whimsical hand-painted floor treatment. The kitchen nods to England's Royal Pavilion (in Brighton) with its vibrant green tile and range, whimsical lanterns that dangle overhead, and eighteenth-century fretwork table that has been repurposed as a kitchen island. The dining room references Laudrée in Paris, a favorite spot, and shines with pieces culled from antiques stores in Minneapolis (the vintage Murano glass chandelier) and eBay (Venetian-style dining chairs).

A living room in Beverly Hills once crafted by iconic designer Elsie de Wolfe was our stepping-off point for the slightly formal sitting room, where a custom Gracie scenic wallpaper pairs with bespoke faux-bamboo molding, gilt mirrors, and painted furniture. A former pantry is now a bar, aka the India Bar, complete with antique portraits and photographs of maharajas, culled from various trips to Rajasthan, who stare down onto chilled martinis and Gin Rickeys (the house cocktail), served neat. Then there is the pistachio-green, lattice-clad sunroom; the garden entrance that tips its hat to late heiress Bunny Mellon and her garden-inspired sensibility; and the opium den–like retiring room. . . .

Upstairs, the master bedroom nods to England's historic Kelmarsh Hall, the onetime home of interior design force Nancy Lancaster, while another channels a certain Cotswolds country-inspired charm. And, of course, the Joan Fontaine bedroom incorporates a canopy bed culled from the estate of the famed *Rebecca* actress alongside contemporary art.

The house now plays up its 1930s-era roots with a whimsical, cheeky sense of humor and glittering sophistication. Think timeless black-and-white tiled bathrooms, albeit wallpapered in Palm Beach–inspired prints and painted in pale pink hues. Furnishings are a tad cinematic, and references to classic period films such as *The Thin Man* and *Auntie Mame* are in abundance.

opposite Stepping into the foyer of this North Carolina home is riveting thanks to the hand-painted decorative treatments that envelop the floor, walls, and ceiling. Notice how the decoration isn't pristine or perfect but rather has been scuffed up a tad and intentionally distressed so that it feels original to the home. A tented room finished off with faux tassels and faux-stone walls, perfection! Because the patterns are so bold and rich, the furniture scheme is minimal and lets the room really breathe.

left A hand-painted eighteenth-century English grandfather clock stands tall in the gorgeously detailed foyer. The clock's front references patterns found throughout the house on other painted furniture pieces.

below Use pattern to make hallways, foyers, stairs, and other pass-through spaces sparkle. This mural's tents, topiaries, and languid games of croquet are favorite motifs inspired by murals we spotted in England.

opposite The pattern motifs that take center stage in the foyer continue through the home by traveling up the staircase and into the home's second floor courtesy of a mural inspired by the twentieth-century English painter Rex Whistler. Create an overall pattern vision for your home, then weave the thread throughout. You don't want it to look like you focused on one space and forgot to address that room's relationship with the rest of the house.

211

this page In great English country houses of a
certain period, chinoiserie played an important
role, reflecting the increased trade routes with China
and East Asia. Wallpapers festooned with peony
trees, pagodas, and temples reflected the fascination
with far-off, exotic locales. In the living room, the
chinoiserie wallpaper (with portraits of our three
dogs peeking out) is the anchor pattern for the room.
We layered in a Chinese mirror above the mantel,
patterned upholstery in the form of armchairs and
tabouret stools (in colors pulled from the wallpaper),
and a reverse-painted, mirrored coffee table. The
custom wallpaper is inspired by the sitting room at
Kelmarsh Hall (home of our idol, Nancy Lancaster).

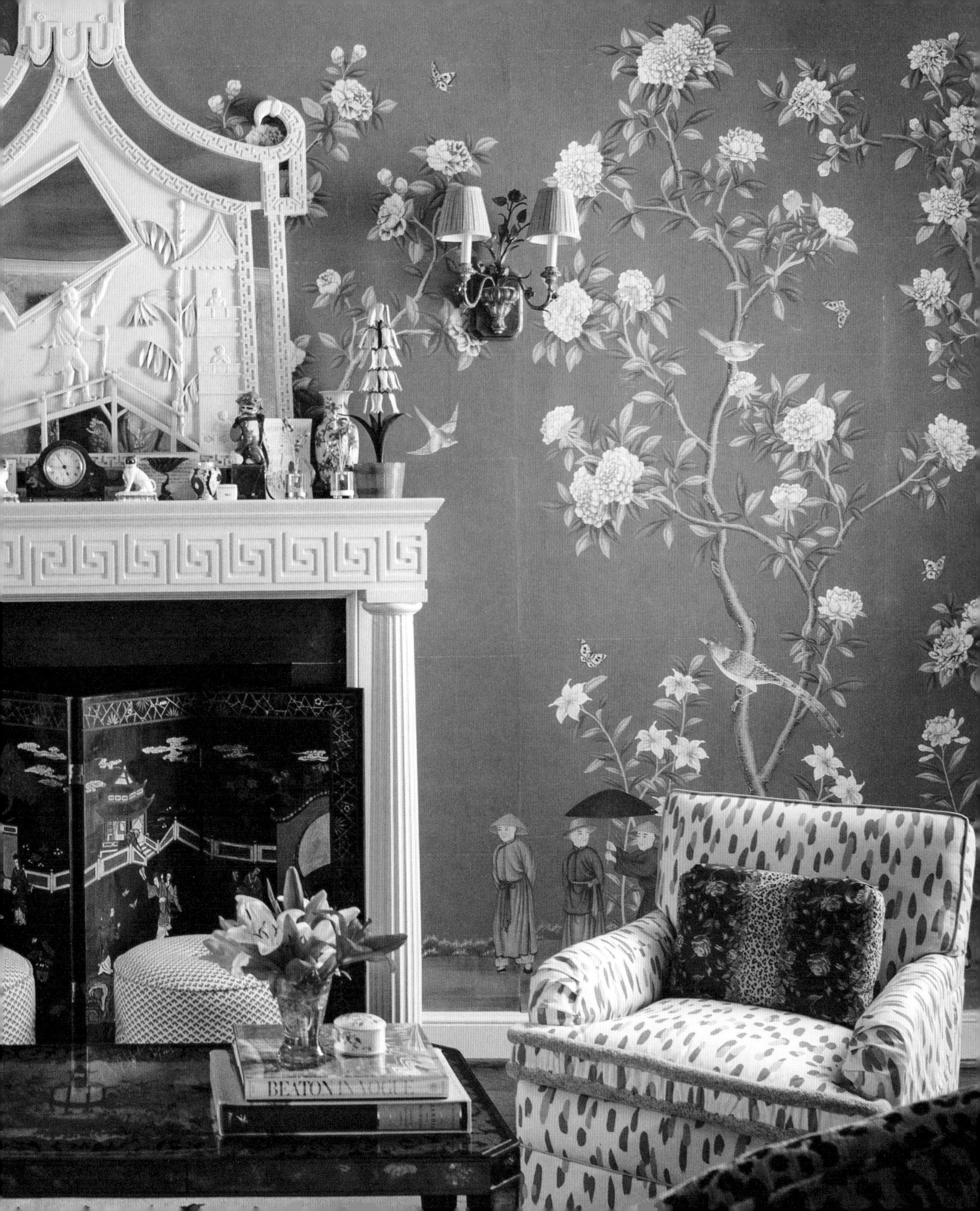
BEATON IN VOGUE

Dream big and create interiors that pack a (patterned) punch.

left Pattern need not always be bold: A subtle woven white-on-white pattern on the sofa, trimmed with pale green silk welt (pulled from the room's striped silk drapes) and matching Greek key tape, adds a cool sophistication to the living room. Mix in a few decorative pillows, including a works-everywhere pair of animal prints, for the perfect finishing touch.

above The graphic qualities of the mantel—original to the home—play up a Greek key motif that appears on the exterior of the home as well as on the hand-painted floors within the foyer. The custom Chinese mirror above the mantel accentuates the bespoke chinoiserie wallpaper.

opposite An antique Chinese rug pairs with the scenic wallpaper and brings a timeless storyline to life. Black furnishings add just the right amount of neutral to allow the room's patterns to truly sing.

left In the den, the striped upholstered walls (yes, they are covered in fabric) create the structure that allows for the bold pattern play—from the suzani decorative pillows and the vintage paintings to the tasseled lampshades and colorful accessories scattered across the coffee table. Jasper approves heartily.

opposite On the den's daybed, vintage pillows, including Turkish suzanis and whimsical needlepoints, work together thanks to the conversation between colors, especially yellow and red, found in the various patterns and exotic florals.

opposite Chinese motifs carry into the den through the use of an antique English tole and blanc de chine chandelier, the custom ceiling ornamentation, and exotic accessories such as the wood pagoda. A taste of India—in the form of the upholstered screen—suggests the romance of travel. The room's bold color scheme, a mix of reds, blues, yellows, browns, and grays, makes the small space feel larger.

left Animal prints work anywhere. Repeat that, friends. Animal prints work anywhere. Here, a brown zebra-like pattern combined with a paisley stripe revs up a sleek slipper chair. The chair's bright peacock blue welt ties back to the color of the den's built-in bookcases.

above Items collected on our travels fill the shelves of an antique pine cabinet in the den. Pick up treasures as you journey through life rather than scooping up new accessories en masse. The pieces that you display will tell a story and remind you of adventures further afield.

Mix and match the upholstery on dining chairs and watch your guests' eyes light up. A good decor scheme should surprise and delight.

this page A candy box of pattern (think famed macaron maker Ladurée in Paris) creates a European-style fantasy where vintage yellow-hued floral wallpaper pairs with pink and blue bonbons of color. The chairs once inhabited our dining room in Brooklyn (see Chapter 1) and are now covered in durable, Jordan almonds–hued leather. An antique Murano glass chandelier sparkles overhead. Custom lattice paneling wraps around the room and echoes the lattice pattern on the dining table while a vintage needlepoint rug strikes an exuberant note underfoot.

opposite Lighting offers another opportunity to add pattern to a room. Here, an antique Murano glass chandelier brings candy-colored florals and tassel adornments into the dining room mix. The colors of the chandelier reference the pink and blue hues found upon the leather-upholstered dining chairs.

below Needlepoint, on throw pillows, seating, and rugs, lends this sophisticated home's grand rooms a comfortable and relaxed quality, inviting guests to kick back and enjoy.

right A solid silk drapery panel in the dining room gets its groove on with vine-leaf-patterned trim that adds just the right touch of embellishment.

following spread, left Outfit your kitchen the way you would furnish any room in your house, and remember, kitchen cabinets can be furniture pieces. Here, a repurposed antique George IV mahogany library cabinet has become a china cupboard. The island is an eighteenth-century Chinese Chippendale-style console table that we had raised to counter height. The table's fretwork embellishments work back to many of the decorative treatments found throughout our home. The woven-grass dog basket, a favorite of our pups Amy Petunia and Weenie, hails from Africa.

following spread, right Patterned china makes a bold impact within the kitchen's antique library cabinet. As Mother always said, "Use it or lose it." Bust out the good china frequently to set a pattern-rich table. The cabinet's rich blue interior allows the china patterns to really pop.

left Embrace color and pattern in the kitchen, dear friends! Here, a lattice-patterned wallpaper on the ceiling speaks to the garden theme that carries through the home, while floor-to-ceiling tile in various styles channels a hint of *Downton Abbey*. Layer in a yellow retro-style refrigerator and pale green range for yet another spirited dash of color.

opposite Cool green hues carry into the kitchen thanks to the exuberant tile that mixes modern subway-style shapes in green and white with Chinese lattice–inspired trim and antique floral squares picked up on a trip to Portugal. Takeaway: Tile need not be clinical and boring.

opposite A bold yellow sofa wrapped with blowsy, spring-kissed peony blossoms anchors the sunroom's seating area and helps to soften the room's slate floor. Drapery in an overscale palm leaf print frames the windows. The ceiling's lattice-pattern fabric also makes an appearance in the cushions on a pair of vintage rattan chairs. The antique chinoiserie chandelier overhead—along with the pagoda-shaped lamp behind the sofa—carries the Asian theme into the room. What ties everything together? A single color: green, the same color that makes everything in nature blend so beautifully.

right Take an ornate table lamp and give the accompanying shade an equally effusive trim. Here, an Asian gent tops off his ensemble with look-at-me fringe on a black silk pleated shade. The shade's tip-top terrific trim is composed of colors found in the courtly gentleman's colorful dress.

229

right A tented sunroom offers an inviting, sun-kissed spot in which to read and sip a glass of rosé wine. The room's garden theme carries from the outdoors in, thanks to custom lattice-pattern panels that we used to screen the windows and a mix of leafy luxe fabrics that all share a green hue. The verdant potted geraniums and citrus trees bring the added joy of scent into the mix.

LIVING WELL
IS THE
BEST REVENGE

Display items that you have collected on your travels that have meaning and that will whisk you back to a sunny day on the beach or a bustling market in Europe.

left A fretwork étagère that once anchored the guest bedroom in the Madcaps' Brooklyn row house (see Chapter 1) has morphed into a snow-white looker decked out with floral-themed vintage and antique accessories. If you love plants but don't have a green thumb, look to flea markets and antiques shops for flowers crafted of porcelain or metal (aka tole) to bring a low-maintenance look home. PS We love the way that the shelf's lattice framework echoes the lattice-pattern fabric on the sunroom ceiling.

above Lattice and leafy luxe come together thanks to the unifying shade of green. Pick a color, then go up and down the color scale; as long as the eye registers an overall tone, your interior scheme is golden.

above A painted cupboard sits against scenic
wallpaper; the upholstered wall arching overhead
transforms a once-knackered corner into a knockout.

right Classic sophistication meets action-packed
pattern in the master bedroom. Pale gray hues
punctuated with soft pinks and aquas are the
dominant color theme, and a layered pattern plan of
florals and graphics builds on this foundation. Mix in
a wallpaper mural, whimsical pelmets atop the window
treatments, striking bedding, and trim-wrapped
lampshades for a room that is engaging and anything
but cookie cutter. Note the grass-cloth wallpaper on
the ceiling and the arched, upholstered niche that
embraces the bed and creates a cozy, inviting nook.

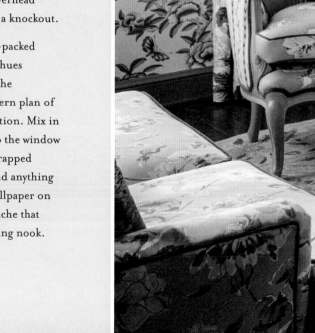

left Hand-painted details on the master bedroom's canopy bedposts mix with striped bed hangings and punchy coral-hued bauble trim. The bed, purchased at auction, had a delicate hand-painted floral design; we had a decorative painter add the Chinese-style figures. The figures are based on those found on the wallpaper panels behind the bed.

below The florals from the bed and floor leap onto a rolled-arm vintage bench that is a favorite perch for the dogs. The jaunty green welting adds the perfect finishing touch. Good welting is next to godliness.

opposite From the floor to the ceiling, florals, florals, and more florals blossom in the master bedroom. When pairing floral fabrics, think about color and style similarities, just as you would when arranging flowers in a vase. The master bedroom's mix is composed primarily of blossoms in shades of pink and coral and all tempered by soft, soothing gray.

left In keeping with the aesthetic of a furnished room rather than a utilitarian space, the bath's vanity was crafted from an eighteenth-century English chest of drawers. The mirror over the vanity is a vintage chinoiserie design, and the sconces on either side of the mirror are vintage finds. Floor-length draperies in a green abstract pattern with bold berry-colored grosgrain ribbon banding complete the look.

below A close-up of the eighteenth-century Chinese panel (picked up for a song at auction) that was slotted into the mahogany frame of the master bathroom's floating tub.

opposite The master bathroom has a decidedly living room vibe. An eighteenth-century chinoiserie panel fills the front of the custom mahogany tub surround, while a vintage Chinese area rug stands in for the traditional bath mat. The walls are papered in a vintage Palm Beach–style floral wallpaper and the ceiling in a textured green grass cloth.

PROJECT
THE BIG COVER UP

THE MADCAPS CANNOT THINK UP ENOUGH NEW WAYS to add detail to upholstery. Beige linen? Never. Well, maybe beige linen with various welts and covered buttons and a floral pattern on the reverse and some bullion fringe and a splash of rick-rack. Take those tired furnishings and reupholster them right this very second! Wait, you don't have an upholsterer in your arsenal? Turn to Calico, friends, as they can reupholster anything—they are not just a fabric or sewing-machine shop as you might have assumed. With their help, the Madcaps crafted a wonderful armchair in a vintage botanical-cum-stripes fabric that we purchased on eBay and welted in rich aqua with a luxe Greek key trim. The result simply sizzles.

With a little help from an upholsterer, you can turn vintage needlepoint pillows (or other needlepoint and embroidered pieces that strike your fancy) into seat covers as we did here. Everyone who comes by to play canasta and a rubber of bridge will comment on your card table chairs! A kicky welt adds another layer of detail.

The back of a chair is just as important as the front, and pattern can really play a big role in giving importance its due. Here, a painterly trellis backs up a vintage Venetian-style armchair with its stunning floral blossoms and bold welting treatment. Green holds the candy land together, and the lattice pattern and blooms bring the garden theme to life.

Think of trim as your new best friend. Here, a vintage armchair boasts a frothy brush fringe edge that adds just that right kick to the upholstery paired with a vintage floral-meets-animal print decorative pillow. Trim comes in every color and frothy goodness imaginable, from grosgrain ribbon (a Madcap Cottage staple) to pom-pom, tassels, brush fringe, and more.

bonus idea

QUILT TRIP The Madcap Cottage gents are crazy about quilting the upholstery on chairs, sofas, pillows—well, anything really—to make a particular pattern, such as a floral, really stand out. How do you create this look? Ask your seamstress to quilt your fabric of choice before it goes to your upholsterer or pillow workroom. It's that simple. This chair has been quilted around the floral bouquets to make them really bloom in abundance, while a vintage floral fabric wraps the exterior of the arm and armrests.

TRADE SECRETS

faux sure

We decided to create an entry that felt tented with heaps of drama, so we turned to a decorative painter to bring our idea to life. And look at the patterned result! Simply heaven. Stepping inside this home is like entering a folly plucked from the Royal Pavilion in Brighton, England. If you have the talent—or you know someone who does—why not try a similar trompe l'oeil treatment in your own home, perhaps on a piece of furniture that you find in a vintage shop? Or, if you are more daring, amp up the drama in a powder room, where a vivacious pattern will make the room feel far more voluminous.

lattice and lovage

Trellis is a classic interior design motif, both indoors and out. Thank design force Elsie de Wolfe, aka Lady Mendl, one of our style icons, for bringing the classic French treatment back to life in the early twentieth century. In the dining room, the Madcaps added depth and pattern to the walls courtesy of custom fretwork designed to fit the dimensions of the room. Our terrific contractor placed the pieces and attached them onto the walls. Note how we used silk cording against the vintage chinoiserie wallpaper to add even more visual interest.

trim is in

Trim really is in, folks, and we cannot get enough of it. Whether rick-rack, welting, pom-poms, or bullion fringe, the Madcaps are mad for trim, and you should be, too. Frankly, the Madcaps cannot think of a place where trim shouldn't be used! Think of trim as the jewelry on a furnishing or curtain panel or decorative pillow. Here, bead trim adds the perfect punctuation—as well as a jolt of color—on rich striped silk curtains in the living room.

happy accidents

Let's say you have a design plan all mapped out, but then
you discover a fabric that you cannot live without or you
find a vintage pattern that's absolute perfection hidden
under layers and layers of wallpaper. The Madcaps call this a
"happy accident," and design, like life, isn't black and white.
Why not take these moments and make the most of them?
During our own High Point, North Carolina, renovation,
we had the wallpaper in our living room stripped, and we
discovered a "ghosted" pattern that remained after we took
down almost six layers of paper. The remaining pattern
looked almost like a luxe Fortuny fabric from Italy, rich
with grays and tans, and we decided to keep it instead of
wallpapering over it as originally planned. The "paper"
channels the rich history of our home and looks amazing!

WHY DON'T YOU

TRANSFORM ANY SURFACE INTO AN
architectural masterpiece by applying trellis fretwork and
plaster medallions (these hail from Chicago's century-
old Decorators Supply). Embellish the ceiling in your sitting
room or den for pure Hollywood glamour. Think silvery
wallpaper that catches the light and other delicious details that
can take this much-overlooked space and give it new life.
And not just a new life, but a new life high in the Hollywood
Hills with a fabulous sports car parked out front.
Dream it and make it happen.

"In restoring a house one must first realize its period, feel its personality, and try to bring out its good points."

—NANCY LANCASTER

YOU OUGHT TO KNOW
NANCY LANCASTER

THE CLASSIC ENGLISH COUNTRY-HOUSE look that we revere today was hardly the invention of the *Downton Abbey* set: Instead, thank Anglo-American designer Nancy Lancaster—a Richmond, Virginia, native (see her ancestral home, Mirador, bottom)—for combining the English aesthetic with an easy-breezy, relaxed American vibe. Think layering, chintz, fresh-cut flowers, ancestral portraits, furnishings culled from various time periods, and comfortable seating. "Pleasing decay" is what the equally important John Fowler, Lancaster's partner in the seminal interior design firm Colefax & Fowler, called the style. The Madcaps have been lucky enough to visit several of Lancaster's former country homes in England, including the incredible Kelmarsh Hall (middle, black and white) and the closed-to-the-public Ditchley Park (top), the inspiration for the Madcap Cottage embroidered print fabric of the same name. The visits were little short of awe inspiring. "It was like visiting a design-minded Lourdes and the Taj Mahal and Paris in the 1920s all rolled into one amazing adventure," says John. To capture the Lancaster sensibility for yourself without having to rent a car—and taking out a hedge! (Yes, that was us in the Avis rental. Ask us about *that* one sometime.)—you might have paid a visit to the Colefax & Fowler design outpost-cum-shop on Brook Street in the heart of London's Mayfair neighborhood, but it moved last year to a nondescript space in Pimlico. We would walk into this sanctum sanctorum and then paw about. Lancaster's famous yellow sitting room (middle) sat upstairs, but then there was the courtyard with its fishpond and the heaps of ideas scattered about the numerous rooms on two levels.

OUR STYLE

If you want an interior that looks like a brand name, that's not us. If you dream of a house that looks like a museum and has spaces that are off limits and all-white living rooms that are only for special occasions, that's not us, either. But if you seek an interior that perfectly captures YOUR brand, style, and sensibility, give us a call.

THE MADCAP COTTAGE GENTS FOUNDED OUR DESIGN FIRM WITH THE FOLLOWING MANDATE:
Create environments that are accessible, sophisticated, and—always, always—perfectly tailored to our clients' wants and needs. Think bespoke: No two of our projects are anything alike from top to toe. The Madcap gents craft living, breathing spaces that are exceptionally comfortable and anything but stuffy. If a room isn't used—and often—that's a sign of design gone wrong.

The Madcaps cull inspiration from our travels, from books we read, from vintage films, and from our passion for adventure. We love pops of color and pattern; we are a little English in our quirky, witty sensibility, but we also celebrate an easy-breezy American vibe; and we firmly believe in traditional with a twist, modern with a splash of the classic, an appreciation of history, and a celebration of a life well lived. Global. Glamorous. Exceptional details. Unexpected moments. A storyline captured and crystallized, then brought to life.

Most importantly, working with us is fun! We love what we do, and we want you to enjoy the ride, too. We aren't fussy, but we are precise and believe in fantastic underpinnings. We don't care about price tags: Good design can be found at every price point. It is not about a dollar amount, but rather about a point of view.

So curl up with a glass of red wine on your Madcap living room sofa; pile on the dogs and the kids and the stacks of magazines and good books; and live life in a home that is quintessentially YOU!

A few of the Madcap Cottage gents' favorite go-to sources to bring your pattern-play vision to life.

IT'S ALL ABOUT HUE

The Madcap Cottage gents love Farrow & Ball (F&B), the English paint company, with its tremendous hues and finishes. Think Arsenic No. 214 (yes, truly!)—a lively sage green that has become a Madcap Cottage staple. F&B is expensive but worth it! Our Brooklyn brownstone floors were painted in F&B, and the finish lasted for years. Today, Farrow & Ball is a quite-known entity and has even become a verb in England. "You 'Farrow & Ball-ed' your home, I see." We also love certain Benjamin Moore formulations, especially those from their Historical Colors selections and WILLIAMSBURG Color Collection. Classic colors never go out of style.

LET'S TAKE FLIGHT

Here are a few of the Madcap Cottage gents' favorite destinations for design inspiration (granted, we still have a lot of the world left to see!):

LISBON, PORTUGAL: *Crumbling and glorious, amazing azulejo tiles and mosaic sidewalks, cheap and chic. Go now before it's overrun.*

SEVILLE, SPAIN: *The tiles, the palaces, the scent of orange blossoms filling the air, the Moorish influences, and the flamenco!*

DES MOINES, IOWA: *From the John and Mary Pappajohn Sculpture Park to the Salisbury House & Gardens and Des Moines Art Center to the vibrant dining scene, and world-class buildings from the likes of David Chipperfield, Renzo Piano, and other architects, this oft-overlooked city is a winner.*

TOKYO, JAPAN: *Retail inspiration heaven. And amazing hotels.*

LONDON, ENGLAND: *Our home away from home. Liberty for the patterns, dinners at the Colony Grill Room, shopping on Lamb's Conduit Street, and long weekends at the whimsical Ham Yard Hotel.*

ANTIGUA GUATEMALA, GUATEMALA: *Secret gardens, terraces, patios, and romantic hostelries.*

SARASOTA, FLORIDA: *The perfect walking downtown with heaps of great restaurants and culture, all looking onto a postcard-perfect bay.*

JODHPUR AND JAIPUR, INDIA: *Transformative, transfixing. Either you love India, or you hate it.*

MEXICO CITY, MEXICO: *Beyond chic. Fantastic, cutting-edge museums, glorious eateries, stunning hotels, and a historic city center packed with action and pure theater.*

SAINT PETERSBURG, RUSSIA: *The royal palaces that ring the city, the low-slung architecture, the topsy-turvy history.*

PAPER CHASE

Did you know that Robert Allen will take our Madcap Cottage for Robert Allen @Home fabrics and back them so that they can be hung like wallpaper? Well, now you do! But beyond our own collections, we love Thibaut and York Wallcoverings, both American staples that have heaps of style and are beautifully priced.

ART FOR ART'S SAKE

Think photographs, vintage prints, contemporary works of art, and your children's paintings! Collect great artwork from various media, then find a local frame store you can work with to bring your style to life. Try fun matting treatments and frame options that perfectly capture a sensibility.

If you need art in an instant, here are a few favorite sources:

ART.COM

THE CONDÉ NAST COLLECTION

EBAY

CUT FROM THE SAME CLOTH

The Madcap Cottage for Robert Allen @Home fabric collection is available at trade showrooms globally and at Calico outposts from coast to coast. The Madcap florals, geometrics, neutrals, and graphics are also available at these wonderful retailers:

ROSEGATE DESIGN, *Birmingham, Alabama*

CYNTHIA EAST FABRICS, *Little Rock, Arkansas*

GOOD GOODS, *Darien, Connecticut*

PATRICIA SPRATT FOR THE HOME, *Old Lyme, Connecticut*

EILEEN & TAYLOR, *Westbrook, Connecticut*

FABRIC GALLERY, *Miami, Florida*

FABRICS & FURNISHINGS, *Conyers, Georgia*

DECORATING MART, *Marietta, Georgia*

GRIFFON DECORATIVE FABRICS, INC., *Carmel, Indiana*

P. TREE TEXTILES, *Baton Rouge, Louisiana*

NELL HILL'S, *Kansas City, Missouri*

FABRICLAND, *North Plainfield, New Jersey*

ZARIN FABRICS, *New York, New York*

FRONT DOOR FABRICS, *Charlotte, North Carolina*

DEXTER FURNITURE, *Raleigh, North Carolina*

FABRIC FARMS, *Hilliard, Ohio*

FABRIC DEPOT, *Portland, Oregon*

AUBUSSON HOME, *Wayne, Pennsylvania*

FOREST LAKE FABRIC CENTER, *Columbia, South Carolina*

CAROLINA FABRICS & INTERIORS, *Greenville, South Carolina*

THE FABRIC HOUSE, *Nashville, Tennessee*

PLUSH FABRIC–HOME INTERIORS, *Cedar Park, Texas*

U-FAB INTERIORS, *Charlottesville and Richmond, Virginia*

WILLIAMS & SHERRILL, *Richmond, Virginia*

BAZAAR HOME DECORATING, *Waukesha, Wisconsin*

RAISING THE BAR

Create a perfect bar, friends, for a fabulous cocktail-crafting assortment that channels pattern aplenty. Not to mention offering the perfect mix of libations. Here's the Madcap Cottage go-to list:

ROSÉ, *especially Bandol*

APEROL SPRITZ, *a traditional Venetian libation (Aperol, Prosecco, and a splash of soda water)*

CHAMPAGNE, PROSECCO, OR CAVA: *Think dry.*

TITO'S HANDMADE VODKA

GRAND MARNIER

SCHWEPPES ORIGINAL BITTER LEMON SODA

WHISKEY: *Brown liquor is always quicker*

GIN: *Sipsmith, The Botanist, and Hendrick's*

FABULOUS OLIVES

VINTAGE BAR ACCESSORIES

COCKTAIL UMBRELLAS

A CLASSIC COCKTAIL MANUAL, *such as* The Savoy Cocktail Book *by Harry Craddock (Girard & Stewart)*

BEDTIME STORIES

Invest in good bed linens, period. You spend a huge portion of your life in bed, so why not make that time marvelous? Think quality over quantity. Favorites:

THE MADCAP COTTAGE FOR HSN COLLECTION *offers stellar design (patterns aplenty!) at an affordable price available exclusively on HSN.com*

D. PORTHAULT AND FRETTE: *Expensive, but stunning!*

MARTHA STEWART HOME COLLECTION *at Macy's*

THE BIG COVER-UP

Think of an upholsterer—a key part of any interior design scheme—like a good

dry cleaner or cobbler. Turn to our friends at Calico, who can reupholster and custom craft anything you need. Find a fabulous vintage chair at a flea market with good bones, and let Calico reupholster the piece with the fabrics that you find at any of their outposts from coast to coast (and, yes, they have the entire Madcap Cottage for Robert Allen @Home fabric collection!).

VIVA VINTAGE

Gang: Look to vintage finds for fabulous scale and proportion, something that's often quite hard to come across in today's overscale, oversize creations. Peruse flea markets, estate sales, and roadside offerings. OK, yes, we will dumpster dive. A few favorites:

ANTIQUE & DESIGN CENTER OF HIGH POINT: *The furniture capital of the world, High Point, North Carolina (the Madcap Cottage gents' hometown), hosts the twice-annual High Point Market. Sadly, most of the show is only open to the trade, but there are certain areas that the public can visit, such as the stellar Antique & Design Center. Be sure to visit Stephanie Freitas and Denise Eckert of the Sweetwood Collection, a favorite source.*

ANTIQUE MARKET PLACE: *Find the Madcap Cottage gents' collection of antique and vintage finds, all under one roof in Greensboro, North Carolina, and all packed with heaps of wit and fun.*

BRIMFIELD ANTIQUE SHOW: *The thrice-annual antiques extravaganza in western Massachusetts offers endless fields full of design inspiration. Just get there early before the teams from Ralph Lauren and Anthropologie cart off all of the good stuff.*

ST. PETERSBURG, FLORIDA: *Jason grew up in Tampa, Florida, and nearby St. Pete was always quiet when he was a kid. Well, no more! Explore the antiques scene on Central Avenue that stretches for over a mile. Afterward, head to nearby St. Pete Beach for a cool cocktail paired with a stellar sunset.*

Other favorite spots include the Rose Bowl Flea Market in Pasadena, California; the antiques outposts in Des Moines, Iowa, such as the Brass Armadillo Antique Mall; the antiques shops on Route 1 in southern Maine, aka the Maine Antique Trail; the Original Round Top Antiques Fair in South Carmine, Texas; Bermondsey Antiques Market, Portobello Road, Covent Garden Market, and Spitalfields Traders Market in central London; and any of the Renninger's shows.

HOTEL STORIES

The Madcap Cottage gents derive heaps of inspiration from travel, so here's a list of hotels that have left us reeling.

CLARIDGE'S: *Our favorite hotel in London, hands down. History? Check. Amazing design? Check. Glorious service and the perfect location? Check. Who would have thought that Edwardian architecture paired with an art-deco overlay would come together seamlessly, but it all works. Pattern mixing at its best. Be sure to check out the toilets: The basement-level Gents' is a stunner, so we assume that the Ladies' is tip-top, too.*

TAJ LAKE PALACE: *The most stunning hotel we have yet to visit. A former maharaja's palace smack in the center of Lake Pichola in Udaipur, India. Private. Perfect. Exceptional.*

THE POINT RESORT: *An ultra-luxe, intimate escape high in New York's Adirondacks. Save your pennies for a weekend away at this former Rockefeller camp, where the relaxed service is off the charts. Cross-country skiing with a Champagne picnic lunch in a heated cabin? No problem. Truffled popcorn and a movie at 3 A.M.? But of course! It's like staying in the chicest of homes.*

SOFITEL WINTER PALACE: *Step inside this historic hotel overlooking the Nile River in Luxor, Egypt, and you wouldn't be surprised to find Agatha Christie peeking out from behind a potted palm. A throwback oasis of calm and luxe. And plenty of volupté, too!*

FIRMDALE HOTELS: *Hoteliers Tim and Kit Kemp craft bespoke magic with their highly unique hotel group that stretches from London to New York. Patterns and colors take center stage at favorite outposts such as the Charlotte Street and Ham Yard hotels.*

THE BEVERLY HILLS HOTEL: *If only for the pink walls, cabana stripes, and Dorothy Draper wallpaper.*

THE GREENBRIER: *Dorothy Draper and Carleton Varney designed this colorful, pattern-packed, sprawling resort in West Virginia. Amble from room to room and lap up the glorious decor and theatricality.*

THE UPPER HOUSE: *A sleek, chic oasis in the center of bustling, frenetic Hong Kong. Stunning interiors and unobtrusive, perfect service. And the views from the floating tubs—heaven!*

THE GRITTI PALACE: *A classic on the Grand Canal in Venice, Italy. Rooms are beyond our pay scale (although we checked in once), but we settle into the mirror-and-Murano-glass–bedecked Bar Longhi and fall into dreamland.*

THE CARLYLE: *A New York City classic with Dorothy Draper vestiges and crisp elevator men. Visit Café Carlyle and Bemelmans Bar. In a city that should have world-class hotels—but really doesn't—the Carlyle tops our list.*

THE COLONY HOTEL: *A bastion of WASP style, fabulously tatty chic in Kennebunkport, Maine. Plus, fantastic floral cabbage-rose wallpaper in the rooms! Croquet, horseshoes, and shuffleboard paired with a Southside cocktail—sign us up!*

MENA HOUSE HOTEL: *Wake up to views of the pyramids—literally, they're across the street—from this historic former hunting lodge in Giza, Egypt, just outside of Cairo. Be sure to stay in the historic building, not the newer wings. We even wore turbans at dinner.*

THE MOUNTAIN BROOK INN: *A charming country motel in the Catskill Mountains near our very own cozy cottage, this hostelry boasts comfortable, atmospheric rooms overlooking a raging brook. Gary, the owner, is the perfect host and delivers breakfast in a basket every morning. On Saturday nights, the inn's living room transforms into a rollicking dinner party with a set menu (and spot-on wine list).*

MUSEUM MILE

The Madcaps are inveterate museumgoers and glean so much inspiration from cultural institutions around the world. Here are a few of our favorite museum must-visits:

THE FRICK COLLECTION: *An intimate New York gem in a city of blockbuster exhibits and crowds.*

THE ISABELLA STEWART GARDNER MUSEUM: *This Boston spot never changes. The central garden with its skylight and fern-draped mosaic floor is heaven.*

DES MOINES ART CENTER: *An unexpected gem designed by Eero Saarinen, I. M. Pei, and Richard Meier.*

THE METROPOLITAN MUSEUM OF ART: *For the Wrightsman Galleries for French Decorative Arts, among all of the other splendor in Manhattan.*

NATIONAL PORTRAIT GALLERY, LONDON: *Free and fabulous. The perfect location and a great place to stop into weekly without having to queue up as one must at the Met or MoMA in New York. Walk right in and enjoy.*

THE WALLACE COLLECTION: *An unsung hero off Oxford Street in London with gems from Fragonard, Hals, Titian, and more. A great restaurant, too.*

DULWICH PICTURE GALLERY: *It's well worth the Tube and bus rides to this charming gallery tucked into leafy Dulwich, South London.*

V&A MUSEUM: *The best museum in London (and anywhere, for that matter) for design aficionados. The furniture galleries, the Great Bed of Ware, Tipu's Tiger, and the porcelain collections.*

MUSEO NACIONAL DEL PRADO: *Goya. And Velázquez. In the heart of Madrid.*

EL ESCORIAL: *Severe and splendid in Spain.*

MUSÉE CARNAVALET: *A charming former pair of hôtels particuliers in the Marais district that tells the history of Paris.*

THE GETTY: *For the gardens and for Richard Meier's architecture that floats high above Los Angeles.*

EL MUSEO JUMEX: *A cutting-edge and riveting collection in Mexico City.*

HOUSE OF LOVE

The Madcaps cannot get enough of great house museums, from the United States to the United Kingdom. Here, just a few of our favorites.

BEAUPORT, AKA THE SLEEPER-MCCANN HOUSE, GLOUCESTER, MASSACHUSETTS: *Our favorite house museum in the United States, hands down. Take in the pale green dining room, the Chinese wallpaper–wrapped China Trade Room, and the views onto Gloucester harbor. Run, now.*

HEARST CASTLE, SAN SIMEON, CALIFORNIA: *William Randolph Hearst's sprawling castle high above the Pacific. Visit if only to see the indoor Roman Pool.*

BILTMORE, ASHEVILLE, NORTH CAROLINA: *The Vanderbilts' great escape. Robber baron exuberance at its finest, all big and bold. But look closely for simple chic elements.*

HILLWOOD ESTATE, MUSEUM & GARDENS, WASHINGTON, DC: *Marjorie Merriweather Post's aerie, filled with Russian luxe, including Fabergé eggs.*

SIR JOHN SOANE'S MUSEUM, LONDON: *A magical oasis of sculptures and whimsy in the heart of London and the former home of the renowned neoclassic architect.*

LEIGHTON HOUSE MUSEUM, LONDON: *The one-time home of Victorian-era painting superstar Lord Leighton, this tucked-away retreat beckons visitors with its glorious Arab Hall.*

ENGLAND'S NATIONAL TRUST PROPERTIES: *Specifically Petworth House and Park, Belton House, and Polesden Lacey, among so many others.*

CHATSWORTH, DERBYSHIRE, ENGLAND: *The ancestral home of the dukes of Devonshire. The best of the best, from the art to the interiors to the gardens. Plus, the spirit of Deborah Mitford Cavendish, Duchess of Devonshire, still permeates the estate.*

RETAIL THERAPY

The Madcap Cottage gents scour the world for the best and brightest retail outposts that offer up the unique and exceptional. For us, England wins hands down. But here are a few of our favorites from both sides of the pond.

THE CONRAN SHOP: *Head to the outpost in charming, village-like Marylebone in the heart of London for an exceptional selection of wares. A great café, too.*

ANTHROPOLOGIE: *For everything from vintage finds to fantastic prints, housewares, and books. Yes, books! (Like this glorious tome you are currently reading, for example.)*

TERRAIN: *The plants-minded nursery-cum-lifestyle store from the brains behind Anthropologie and Urban Outfitters. A great place to shop and eat.*

CALICO: *A one-stop shop for every fabric need under the sun. Custom upholster a chair or sofa and shop an exceptional assortment of fabrics. Have window treatments made or go for bespoke bedding.*

FORTNUM & MASON: *London's unparalleled epicurean-minded department store. Always fresh and fabulous. Even the labels are genius. We love shopping for honey and tea before lunching at 45 Jermyn St. A great spot for tea, too, or a picnic lunch to carry over to nearby Green Park.*

LIBERTY: *A heritage-minded department store in London that celebrates its legacy while constantly thinking fashion-forward. From the iconic Liberty print fabrics to housewares and fashion, this mock Tudor-style emporium always wows us with its ever-changing stock.*

SELFRIDGES & CO: *Cutting edge, smart, editorial, and fresh on London's bustling Oxford Street. From seasonal eateries on the roof to pop-up shops.*

V&A SHOP: *One of the best museum gift shops anywhere in the world at one of the world's best design museums. We head to this London staple for one-off items and stocking stuffers. An exceptional array of wares.*

PATTERN CREDITS

ALMOST EVERY PATTERN IN this book is from the Madcap Cottage for Robert Allen @Home fabric collection, available globally. To learn more about specific patterns and colorways, visit the Madcap Cottage website at www.madcapcottage.com and click on the navigation bar at the top of the home page. Then you can follow our blog, peruse our portfolio, and hang out in print-packed bliss. We look forward to seeing you online!

ACKNOWLEDGMENTS
or Thank You for Stepping on the Ping-Pong Ball!

GANG: WHAT AN ADVENTURE!

The conceptualizing, writing, styling, and photography of *Prints Charming* has been an amazing ride, a gorgeous roller coaster. . . . Yes, that was us cutting out thumbnail images at 3 A.M. to make sure a certain chapter looked just so, running to delis on Manhattan's West Side for peonies to bring a desired detail shot to life, and conjuring up synonyms for "adore," "pops of color," and "inviting" *ad nauseum* over martinis. Forget a village, it took a rollicking, good-time cocktail party to bring this ship to shore. Curious, serious good fun.

As our cinematic heroine Mae West once said, "It's better to be looked over than overlooked," so here's a bottle of champers and a bouquet of tightly bunched tea roses to the following folks who helped make the Madcap Cottage vision a reality. Thank you to our longtime, go-to photographer John Bessler—and his assistant Julian Huarte—for capturing high-octane magic within your lens. Hip-hip to Jay Wilde in Des Moines, Iowa, and Bert VanderVeen in Greensboro, North Carolina, for contributing further stunning visuals. And cin-cin to our agent at Stonesong, Judy Linden, and our editor at Abrams, Shawna Mullen, for your kindness, guidance, virtual love-ins, and ever-present fun: You two are the best! Kudos to Shawna's tireless associates Emma Jacobs and Annalea Manalili for keeping us on the straight and narrow—well, maybe just the narrow. To our indefatigable book designer, Sarah Gifford, and Abrams powerhouse creative director, John Gall, for crafting pure magic. And we wouldn't have hit our marks without the very talented Lacey Howard of Goode Girl Media.

We hope that these two Madcap apples didn't fall so far from the tree, so hugs and kisses to our visionary parents for allowing us to blossom into tempestuous tulips instead of shrinking violets. To our amazing interior design clients—several of whom opened their homes and apartments to us in this book—for believing in our vision and for living with it each and every day. To

Ashley Hicks, Susan Crater, Billie Ayers, and Miry Park. To the incredible team and our dear partners at Robert Allen @Home—among them, Hannah Alderson, Donna Rinaldi, Lucy Maitland, Jennie Wilde, David Lappert, Pam Hausman, and Jana Weill—for taking a chance on two kids from High Point who had prints in their hearts and patterns on their brains. And cheers to Christy Almond and Robert Nachman for inviting us to the table.

We are so lucky to have partnerships with HSN, Calico, and Smith & Noble—not to mention 1stdibs and One Kings Lane: Thank you, dear friends! Hats off to our hero, Carleton Varney. And heaps of dog bones to our pound-rescue posse, Jasper, Weenie, and Amy Petunia: You keep us going with your endless love and ability to always make us smile—even when a photo shoot goes awry or one million words of text is due tomorrow.

A big shout-out to our pals on Instagram and Facebook and to our die-hard blog followers for such support over the years. And thank you to our friends in the media, including Ann Maine, Sophie Donelson, Hatta Byng, David Nicholls, Jill Waage, Stephen Orr, the team at Apartment Therapy, Rachel Hardage, and Eugenia Mikulina. And a nod to Allison Ingram at Condé Nast for going above and beyond on the photo research front.

To Regina Birrenkott for believing in us, and to Elaine for not.

Here's to questioning the status quo, to being kind and humble, to never being boring, and to sprinkling glitter wherever you go.

To never stop dreaming and to always being a kid in a candy store.

To quote an album cover of our favorite band, Wham!, "Make it big."

Or go home.

Just make sure your home is awash in prints and patterns.

xoxo

editor SHAWNA MULLEN

designer SARAH GIFFORD

production manager DENISE LACONGO

Library of Congress Control Number: 2016961375

ISBN: 978-1-4197-2664-4

Printed and bound in China

10 9 8 7 6 5 4 3 2 1

Abrams books are available at special discounts when purchased in quantity for premiums
and promotions as well as fundraising or educational use. Special editions can also be created
to specification. For details, contact specialsales@abramsbooks.com or the address below.

ABRAMS The Art of Books
115 West 18th Street, New York, NY 10011
abramsbooks.com